The
Ten
Commandments
and
Christian
Community

The
10
Commandments
&
Christian
Community

Jay W. Marshall

HERALD PRESS
Scottdale, Pennsylvania
Waterloo, Ontario

Library of Congress Cataloging-in-Publication Data
Marshall, Jay W. (Jay Wade), 1959-
    The Ten Commandments and Christian community / Jay W.
    Marshall
    p. cm.
    Includes bibliographical references (p.).
    ISBN 0-8361-902 7-0 (alk. paper)
    1. Ten commandments—Criticism, interpretation, etc. 2. United
States—Moral conditions. I. Title.
    BV4655.M378 1995
    241.5'2—dc20   95-24084
                                                        CIP

THE TEN COMMANDMENTS AND CHRISTIAN COMMUNITY
Copyright © 1996 by Herald Press, Scottdale, Pa. 15683
    Published simultaneously in Canada by Herald Press,
    Waterloo. Ont. N2L 6H7. All rights reserved
Library of Congress Catalog Number: 95-24084
International Standard Book Number: 0-8361-9027-0
Printed in the United States of America
Book design by Gwen M. Stamm

05 04 03 02 01 00 99 98 97 96 10 9 8 7 6 5 4 3 2 1

To my wife, Judi,
who is keeping
her promise

Contents

Preface

Of all the material in the Old Testament, the Decalogue has been the most influential passage in terms of its effect on modern Western society. Its effects upon our legal systems and businesses are evident. Murder and theft are prohibited. Telling lies is not suitable social behavior in our courts or our communities. In some places, adultery is a crime; occasionally it is used in divorce and child custody suits as a slanderous character trait.

Even the Sabbath law has been influential, resulting in blue laws that regulate Sunday business hours. Only in recent years have lawmakers relaxed these restrictions. Whether intentional or not, such regulations have permeated contemporary law and mores.

The Ten Commandments have also been influential in evaluations of personal piety, especially by individuals who have adopted "passive Christianity" as their expression of faith. In such lifestyles, the letter of these laws becomes a convenient measuring tool for persons who wish to determine their "goodness." If they can claim not to worship little statues, not to use profanity, not to have killed anyone, and so forth, then they have successfully met the standard. Consequently, according to the logic employed, they are moral and faithful people.

We can celebrate the contribution of these ancient laws toward peace and morality in our world. But the Decalogue has more to offer, and Christians need to listen.

First, it can teach us about *commitment*. In a world where mainline denominations continue to report declines in church membership, faith as it is taught in the church apparently requires so little commitment that members can effortlessly fade away from the fold. But for the Decalogue, faith begins with the covenant, and covenants are not taken lightly. They do more than grant privilege. They also usher in responsibilities. In an age when Christians have problems keeping commitments, we can learn from the covenant approach to a relationship with God. It will remind us that faith is to be taken seriously!

Second, it teaches us about an essential part of being a Christian congregation. More than a gathering of people, believers who live and worship together are expected to become a faith community. *Community* is a word being used in many circles. Often it operates as little more than a synonym for a place of comfort, warmth, and fellowship. One certainly hopes to find those things in a faith community, but there must be more to it than that. When we realize how much more encompassing the concept is to biblical faith groups, we then see the deficiency of defining the church's purpose merely as a cozy club.

Before automobiles and superhighways, prior to satellite TV and malls, the church occupied a more centrally located place in the lives of its constituents. Participation in the worship of the congregation was not the only high priority item. For its families, the church was also the religious, social, and sometimes political center.

Now, except for the most dedicated of believers, the church often is located on the periphery of people's social calendars. It is one option among many others and can easily be shuffled around or interchanged with other interests. That in itself will make it difficult for the church to be a community.

Though it is unlikely that the church will ever be the nerve center or social outlet that it once was, it still must discover a way to be more than merely a social or an entertainment option. One appealing alternative is to become a living model of community as God designed it. The faith of individuals in the biblical story was always set within the larger context of community. In contrast, contemporary understandings of faith have fallen prey to the Western fad of individualism promoting a privatized faith that believes it can exist independently of a larger body. But biblical faith was communal. The faith community served as a source of identity. Guidelines for worship, work, and relationships existed. Accountability to those guidelines was expected. Today's church often struggles to maintain that role.

Becoming a real faith *community* may be difficult. Being in community requires living together, trusting each other, and to some degree, depending upon each other. It is a challenge to achieve those things in one to two hours per week. Hence, some say the church has lost the ability to be a real community. But we must not give up hope for at least two reasons. One, it is part of our calling as Christians. Two, the world needs us to show it how a true community looks.

The world has always been changing, but now it seems to change more rapidly. What are the constants? Who can be trusted? What are the criteria for being a good person or Christian who wants to live at peace with God and neighbor? When chaos feels near, where is the support? As society's values change, sometimes in unhealthy ways, where is a model for wholeness and health? One wonderful way the church and Christians can share their faith is to assume leadership in this area. This book on the Ten Commandments is designed to help us begin to address the issue of community from a biblical perspective.

The Ten Commandments

Exodus 20:1-17

And God spoke all these words: "I am the Lord your God, who brought you out of Egypt, out of the land of slavery.

1. You shall have no other gods before me.

2. You shall not make for yourself an idol in the form of anything in heaven above or on the earth beneath or in the waters below. You shall not bow down to them or worship them; for I, the Lord your God, am a jealous God, punishing the children for the sin of the fathers to the third and fourth generation of those who hate me, but showing love to thousands who love me and keep my commandments.

3. You shall not misuse the name of the Lord your God, for the Lord will not hold anyone guiltless who misuses his name.

4. Remember the Sabbath day and keep it holy. Six days you shall labor and do all your work, but the seventh day is a Sabbath to the Lord your God. On it you shall not do any work, neither you, nor your son

or daughter, nor your manservant or maidservant, nor your animals, nor the alien within your gates. For in six days the Lord made the heavens and the earth, the sea, and all that is in them, but he rested on the seventh day. Therefore the Lord blessed the Sabbath day and made it holy.

5. Honor your father and mother, so that you may live long in the land the Lord your God is giving you.

6. You shall not commit murder.

7. You shall not commit adultery.

8. You shall not steal.

9. You shall not give false testimony against your neighbor.

10. You shall not covet your neighbor's house. You shall not covet your neighbor's wife, or his manservant or maidservant, his ox or donkey, or anything that belongs to your neighbor."

Prologue

The Area Code of Faith

All of us know something about the Ten Commandments. We probably cannot name all ten, but along the way we came to believe they were important. We saw them tacked to Sunday school class walls and taught to us as children. We thought that the Ten Commandments, if faithfully kept, could win God's approval for us.

Some good-intentioned believers even insisted that if we broke any one of the Ten Commandments, we had committed the most heinous of crimes. Such disobedience was wrong, and these commandments became the primary measuring stick for Christian morality.

So we became convinced that these ancient laws have something to do with our daily lives—but we are not sure exactly how. North Americans honor the Ten Commandments more by reverence toward them than by actually keeping them. After all, we are constantly bombarded with stories of murder, lying, cheating, stealing, adultery, disrespect for parents—the list could consume several pages!

This book reconsiders the Ten Commandments. We seek to delve beneath the legalistic surface that has covered them and discover the positive, life-giving spirit that remains relevant in our world, even as we speed toward the twenty-first century.

One may wonder if the Ten Commandments merit any attention from Christian believers. They are, after all, part of the Old Testament law, and the apostle Paul taught that Christians had "died to the law" of Moses (Rom. 7:4). Thus we believe that "through Christ Jesus the law of the Spirit of life set me free from the law of sin and death" (8:2), and that "Christ is the end of the law" (10:4). However, Paul also made some positive statements about the law. He called it "holy, and the commandment is holy, righteous and good," and "spiritual" (7:12; 14a). In Romans 3:31, he actually claims to uphold, rather than nullify, the law!

These diverse statements have not gone unnoticed by students of Scripture. Bible scholars' interpretations of Paul's statements regarding the law continue to create controversy and debate. Rather than rehash that debate or attempt to provide an authoritative word on Paul's theology of the law, perhaps there is a more expedient way to address the pertinent question of whether or not the Ten Commandments have any bearing on Christian faith communities.

First, let us acknowledge that hardly anything negative is said about the law by other New Testament writers. Even Jesus himself was not as critical of the law as was Paul. Though Jesus occasionally was accused of breaking the law and offered new interpretations of the law, he also understood his work as fulfilling the law. Jesus as the fulfillment of the law is quite different from Jesus as the negation of the law.

Thus, the Transfiguration (Matt. 17; Mark 9; Luke 9) presents Jesus in conversation with Moses and Elijah, representatives of the Mosaic Law and Hebrew Prophets. And the Gospel of John, directed toward Christian believers, describes how we have received "one blessing after another" (1:16-17, NIV), "grace upon grace" (NRSV). First, the law was given through Moses; then grace and truth came through Christ. So Christians should not be quick to totally dismiss the Old Testament material as worthless.

Equally important to the discussion are Paul's own words to Timothy where he says, "All Scripture is God-breathed and is useful for teaching, rebuking, correcting, and training in righteousness, so that the person of God may be thoroughly equipped for every good work" (2 Tim. 3:16). For Paul, all Scripture certainly included the Old Testament, because at the time of his letter to Timothy, there was little else that the church considered to be Scripture.

In this discussion, the issue is one of "law as source of salvation" versus "law as valuable for instruction." While Christ has done what the law could not do, and while Christians should not seek salvation through the observance of the law, that does not make the Old Testament revelation useless to us. Now that Christ has set us on the path of faith and discipleship, the Old Testament, and especially the Ten Commandments, act like guardrails that help keep us on the right path. There is much that God can teach us through this material!

As we begin the task of uncovering the life-giving principles within these ancient laws, think about the different types of codes that affect you. There are bar codes that appear on merchandise in stores, especially supermarkets. In many instances, they have slowed the checkout process to a snail's pace. If supermarkets offered a "thirty minute or less" checkout guarantee, many of us would eat for free. From the postal service we have zip codes, which are becoming longer and longer, as is the delivery time of the postal service! But zip codes are great because those few numbers somehow direct our mail to the correct neighborhood.

There are tax codes that help decide how much lint we need in our pockets in order to feel like there is something substantial there after April 15. There are dress codes, which are troubling because they change so frequently. Today's acceptable fashions expire more quickly than low-fat milk. There are honor codes. And the Morse code. Even our written alphabet is a code that communicates thoughts and sounds.

Codes rank among the most important things in life. Whether they are identifying something, communicating information, or setting standards, codes help us sort out what is important and what things are valuable. Of the various types of codes available to us, think of the Ten Commandments as an area code.

An area code identifies a particular area, which is larger than a zip code locality. It affects everyone who lives within the boundaries of that area and wishes to be reached by phone. The area code covers all who live in that district, uniting and distinguishing the residents in an odd way. If a person lives outside that area and wishes to communicate by phone with another person inside the area, then one must be aware of that code. Otherwise, the connection cannot be made. Entry into the area by means of the telephone connection is denied, preventing communication and dialogue.

The Ten Commandments together formed a covenant and a code that mapped out an area of accepted beliefs and practices. This code is broad in some ways, but focused in others. If one wanted to understand the Israelites, one had to know something of their code. If one wanted to participate in their community of faith, one had to subscribe to the code. Otherwise, one was left outside the area code, disconnected from those within it.

Do not misunderstand. These commandments are not moral absolutes designed to be read purely from an individual standpoint; nor are they rigid rules merely to be imposed on other people to make them conform to our standard of behavior. Keeping these commands flawlessly until the day you die will not win God's approval. As a code, these commands are about more than keeping people in or out of the area code district. They are about laying the foundation for a solid, stable community of dedicated believers whose most fundamental connection is their belief in and loyalty to the God of the covenant community.

The concept of *covenant community* is another reason Christians should explore afresh our relationship to the Ten Commandments. Much has been written about the fragmented condition of our society and world. Many family units deteriorate at an alarming rate. Racial tensions continue to erupt, even after three decades of intense civil rights movements. Liberation movements continue to produce more minorities than previous generations would have dared imagine. Regional and ethnic conflicts, lying dormant for years, have resurfaced around the world. In the midst of this chaos, and as a response to it, people in many countries are sounding calls to community, beckoning any who will heed them. For any who are interested in responding to this summons, the Old Testament concept of covenant will be useful.

The creation of the Old Testament faith community, which we normally call Israel, was rooted in and defined by the concept of covenant. Many biblical scholars maintain this is the key idea needed for understanding the Old Testament. Indeed, in the Old Testament, it is difficult to find a more foundational or relational term than covenant (Hebrew: *berith*), especially with regard to the Israelite understanding of community. Israel repeatedly used the concept of covenant to understand their history, from the call of Abraham through their return from Babylonian exile. It even influenced their understanding of God and their conception of proper social organization.

From an Old Testament perspective, a covenant was a formal agreement or treaty between two parties. In the Ten Commandments, the agreement was between God and the Israelites. The covenant stated the reason for the agreement, such as what one party had already done for the other: "I am the Lord your God who brought you out of Egypt, out of the land of slavery" (Exod. 20:2). It also described the expectations and responsibilities of the parties involved, such as these commandments describe.

Israel's covenant was *foundational* for its community in the sense that it specified the reason for entering into the agreement with God. God's deliverance of the Israelites was the motivation for entering the covenant, and the foundation for Israel's continuing trust in God. Furthermore, the ensuing commands in Exodus 20, and again in Deuteronomy 5, provided a framework that delineated the essential characteristics and values of the community. God and Israel both expected these commandments to be accepted and shared by those who participated in the covenant.

The Old Testament covenant was *relational* in the sense that it formally established the faith relationship with God. The primary relational characteristic which God brought into the covenant was *khesed*, usually translated as "steadfast love." Besides the accompanying responsibilities and privileges it created, this covenant was characterized by the assurance of God's steadfast love and produced an atmosphere of trust and security. The people knew where they stood with God.

As the covenant described God's actions and intentions in this *khesed*-oriented relationship with the Israelites, it also outlined basic expectations for the participants in their relationship with God and with other Israelites. In short, it outlined acceptable standards for relationships. It defined the area code in which Israelites were expected to reside.

As an example from the Decalogue, members of the covenant community were not only to love the Lord their God; they were also to honor parents, and they were not to murder, nor commit adultery, nor steal, nor lie, nor covet. These guidelines shaped community identity, set community standards, and helped define community boundaries. Accepting the terms of this covenant offered by God established a faith community. Indeed, the goal of the biblical covenant is to create a solid, stable community of faith.

Israel's identity as the people of God was founded on this covenant relationship. As we trace the covenant and its commandments throughout Israelite history, we discover how essential they were to the life of the faith community. Through repetition in Exodus and Deuteronomy, their importance was stressed. Prophetic voices, such as Hosea 4, felt compelled repeatedly to call Israel's attention to their covenant-breaking lifestyles.

Sadly, a major theme in the Old Testament is a demonstration of how Israel's failure to obey the covenant brought drastic consequences. The material of Joshua through Kings attributes the division of the United Kingdom, and the subsequent collapse of the Northern and Southern Kingdoms, to Israel's failure to be faithful to God and the covenant God had made with them.

When the exile ended, the Israelite theologians knew that unless the covenant was kept, history would repeat itself. So the goal of the covenant was to create a stable faith community founded and dependent upon God's grace-filled commandments. Israelite history demonstrates the tragedy that occurs when God's people ignore the covenant and its commands, as well as their eternal hope whenever the covenant is intact.

It would be difficult to overestimate the importance of God's people in ancient Israel, or in any age, living as a faithful covenant community. But what would a genuine community look like in our age? How is it formed? What values shape its foundation? If Christians wish to offer a vision of community as an alternative to other options being peddled like trinkets in a flea market, we must answer those questions.

An obvious source of answers is Scripture and the biblical models it presents. I believe the Ten Commandments, the "area code" for Israel's first post-Egyptian community, have much to teach Christians on the subject of creating a faith community. Beneath each of the terse commands, usually framed as a prohibition, is a positive, life-giving principle whose value endures the tests of time. Those are the life-giving principles that Christians need to rediscover.

For Discussion

1. What codes are most important in the way you order your life? In the way you make decisions? What makes them influential for you?

2. How was the Old Testament covenant foundational and relational for the Israelites? In what ways is the Christian faith foundational and relational for your faith community? Are there any expectations that accompany your participation in the community?

3. Suppose you are responsible for describing the essentials of the code. What basic values of the Christian community would you define as most important? If you are studying this book in a group setting, try to achieve unity on this question.

■▪

I am the Lord your God who
brought you out of the land of
Egypt, out of the house of slavery.
You shall have no other gods
before me.

1

The Gift

A Gracious Covenant

What is the most memorable gift anyone has ever given you? Without doubt, the most wonderful gift I ever received was a Christmas gift during my fifth-grade year. It was a suede leather jacket with fringes dangling from the sleeves and across the back shoulders, like many a cowboy or Native American wears in old Western movies.

This was actually the second such jacket my parents had given me. It was the circumstances under which I lost my first jacket that made this one so special. They gave me the first jacket as autumn approached during my second year of school. It was my absolute favorite piece of clothing. But before the smell of new leather had disappeared, blood stains from a cut received in a school bus accident ruined the jacket.

My school bus overturned on a muddy, country road. I wound up on the bottom of a flesh pile, gasping for air and begging people to get off me. When I was finally freed from that temporary prison, I discovered that I was the loser in a head-to-head confrontation with the school bus window. The window shattered from the impact, and a three-inch gash located just above my left ear flowed like an eternal fountain. That was bad enough, but the blood was spilling all over my jacket.

As a second-grader, I knew next to nothing about fabrics and even less about stains. But I soon learned that blood and suede are not suitable partners. The jacket had to be discarded. I was devastated. For whatever reason, probably because of a tight budget, my parents did not give me another suede leather jacket as a replacement, though I desperately wanted another one. With the passing of time, my grief over losing that jacket faded, but my parents did not forget.

To my surprise, on Christmas morning three years later, one of my gift-wrapped packages contained a new suede leather jacket, with fringes dangling from the arms and across the back shoulders. As I clutched that jacket to my chest, my facial expressions said thank you in a way words could never match. I have received many touching gifts in my lifetime, but none has stirred in me the feelings I felt at that moment. My parents remembered my hurt and pain over losing the original jacket, and they gave the only gift that could erase it.

That is my most unforgettable gift. I am sure you have your own memory, complete with an accompanying story. Those experiences can help us begin to understand the first commandment. Before the giving of the first command, God had observed the hurts and pain of the Israelites, trapped under the weight of slavery. God brought them out from under that mound of oppression and led them to the holy mountain.

In the process of that liberation, God gave Israel several memorable gifts. Israel's freedom, and indeed the very creation of Israel, were gifts of God's love and mercy. Israel was not an accidental or voluntary association based on human intention. It was an intentional creation by God. But the greatest gift that God gave the Israelites was the gift of the covenant. In the covenant, God gave them himself as their Lord.

Verse one begins to unwrap the gift: "And God spoke all these words." The emphasis here is on the word *spoke.* Do you remember the first word spoken by your child, or a younger sibling, nephew, or niece? Even before uttering the first word, the child already communicated with cries, expressions, and gestures. But with the ability to speak came the possibility of more clearly revealing feelings, desires, and messages. Speaking enhances direct communication.

The key word in verse one is "spoke" because with the speaking came revelation. Those words revealed that God desires to be known by those with whom God communicates. This communication was and is a gift from God. Just as important is what God communicated to the Israelites: God said, "I am the Lord *your* God who brought you out of the land of Egypt, out of the land of slavery" (emphasis added). *Your God!* The revelation was a message of choice, of election. It was a message that God had already chosen the Israelites to be a faithful people, and that God had already been active on their behalf.

That teaches us an important initial lesson about this covenant and its commands. These commands have nothing to do with *getting chosen* by God. That choice had already been made. That is what the New Testament calls the gift of grace. And though it is often claimed that the Old Testament lacks grace, that is untrue. In the Old Testament, grace is evident in a gift called covenant.

Some gifts come with the expectation of reciprocation. As God offered them the gift of the covenant, which included God's own commitment to the people, God also expected commitment and loyalty from the Israelites in return. As already indicated, the covenant is not about getting chosen. God had already made that choice. The covenant commands are an invitation to reciprocate the gift by responding to God's choice. In Israel, that *response* became a requirement for all those who wished to live under the area code of this covenant people.

The first command expresses the most important feature of the gift to be reciprocated: "You shall have no other gods before me." This sounds as though God wants to be first in line. The verse may also be translated, "You shall have no other gods besides me." That makes it sound as though God is claustrophobic and does not want to be crowded by the presence of other deities. Another way of reading the verse, "You shall not have any god instead of me," implies that some choice must be made, somewhat like the NBA draft pick—God must be the Number One pick. Actually all three readings are correct and help develop the overall nuance of the verse.

We could think of this command from the perspective of marriage, especially since Hosea uses that imagery to speak of God's relationship with the covenant people. Would you be willing to make a lifetime commitment to someone who said the following? "You can be my spouse, but there will be at least two or three others who have priority over you and receive my attention before you." Or, "I'll marry you, but you'll just be one among many—equal mind you, but there'll be others besides you." Few, if any, would be willing to enter a long-term commitment on those terms. Neither would God.

What God desires of those who wish to live in the area code of the covenant is more along the lines of personal devotion, as described by Robert Fulghum. He told a story about a sergeant major, Nicolai Pestretsov, who was in the Russian army. While he was stationed in Angola, his wife visited him.[1]

While she was there, the Russians were attacked by a group of South Africans. Four Russians were killed and the rest fled, except for Nicolai. He was captured. The military communique said, "Sgt. Major Nicolai Pestretsov refused to leave the body of his slain wife, who was killed in the assault on the village." The South Africans could not believe it. He went to her dead body and stayed there, refusing to leave, though his own life was endangered. He would not run or hide. Perhaps it was because he loved her and wanted to hold her one last time. For whatever the reason, because of his decision to stay with her, he wound up sitting as the lone Russian in a South African jail.

Fulghum says, "Here is to you, Nicolai, wherever you may go and be, for giving powerful meaning to the promises that are the same everywhere; for dignifying that covenant that is the same in any language—for better or for worse, in good times and in bad, in sickness and in health, to love and honor and cherish unto death, so help me God.' You kept the faith; kept it bright—kept it shining."

Though military conflict and the usual goals that motivate war are not to be endorsed, I was touched by this story. Beneath the levels of power that decree shameless destruction and carnage without thought of the effect, human beings discover their lives are shattered and their loyalties challenged. Beneath this sergeant major's military uniform was a loving, committed husband who did an honorable thing in a life-threatening moment. He demonstrated steadfast faithfulness similar to what the first commandment expected in return for the gift of covenant which God gave Israel.

To appreciate that kind of devotion, we need to recognize that most Christians assume there is but one God. They may allow that people of other faiths refer to the one God by different names. But in the era when the Ten Commandments were given, the Israelites believed there were literally lots of gods to choose from. Among the Canaanite gods were Baal and Marduk and Asherah, to name a few, each of whom ruled a particular domain, such as fertility or rain.

There were many stages in the long struggle within Israel to recognize one God. Eight hundred years after the exodus from Egypt, the prophet Isaiah expressed most clearly that there was no other god, only the God of Israel, who is one and unique (as in Isa. 45:14-25). So, the point of the first commandment is not only that one is to cling devotedly to God, but also that among all other possible choices, they (and we) are to choose this God and this God alone.

If we believe that our Christian version of faith calls for anything less from us, then we understand neither God's gift to us, the expectations that accompany it, nor the vital role such commitment plays in the faith community. The first commandment insists that once we have chosen the God of Israel and the God of the Christian faith, we are never to put any other god first or alongside our one true God. We are not to be swayed by what other nations do or whom they worship. The God who has given the gift of the covenant is to be sufficient for all our needs.

If we think that is an irrelevant concern for us since we are monotheists, we are mistaken. Our God is not necessarily the one we claim, but is instead the one whom we follow. Just as Jesus said that wherever our treasure is, so also is our heart (Matt. 6:21), it can be said that wherever our hearts are, there also is our God.

We are tempted to rely upon war and military power to secure our borders, settle our disputes, and keep the peace. If we do so, we are worshiping a warrior God who is created in the national or ethnic image rather than the God who calls us to faith. We may be seduced by advertisements to believe that youth, beauty, and sexuality are to be coveted above all else. If so, we assign values to parts of life that may be different from the values God gives creation. We may succumb to the temptation of thinking that meaning and worth reside in possessions. If so, we betray the One who asked Israel to rely solely on Divine Provision as the people left the holy mountain in pursuit of the Promised Land.

If what we see around us can be trusted, then the old gods continue to live. In that era, they were acknowledged by the Canaanites and attracting Israel; now they have modern names. These gods crave our devotion, but they are as detrimental to a unified faith community now as they were for the Israelites, for one simple reason. They insist that we trust in someone or something other than the God of the covenant to be the giver and sustainer of life.

Jesus' commentary on the first commandment is a vital reminder. A people who chase after all the gods or any gods other than the Lord God, cannot properly reside in the area code created by this covenant. Jesus said, "No one can serve two masters; for a slave will either hate the one and love the other, or be devoted to the one and despise the other" (Matt. 6:24, NRSV).

When given to Moses, the effect of this commandment was to eliminate all other gods as far as Israel was concerned. Other people might still worship them, but not Israel. That would have been an inappropriate response to God's gift.

The effects of not keeping this commandment but still attempting to reside in the same area code, were and still are devastating. Division, disunity, and strife were and are the main problems facing a group who cannot decide whom to serve. A community modeled on the Ten Commandments cannot survive under those conditions because it strips away its very foundation. If Israel was to have a stable faith community, there could only be one

God at the community's center. That Center was the God who had selected them to receive a gift long before Israel had even known such a gift was needed.

If we Christians are to follow the model of community outlined in this area code, one of the things we will need to do is remember our point of origin. We are in the community of faith because God created us and gave us a gift, long before we even knew such a gift was needed. The only proper response to such a gift begins with a commitment to honor and serve the One who is truly the Source of our faith and Center of our life.

■■

The Lord your God shall be
the Source of your life
and the Center of your faith.

For Discussion

1. How does accepting the covenant as a "gift" rather than a "requirement" influence how one understands the Ten Commandments?

2. Assume that such a gift is still offered, both in the teachings about the covenant and through Christ. Then what is the significance of such a gift to you personally, and to the Christian faith community?

3. What current attractions and subsequent loyalties are like "other gods" which entice Christians to forsake the first commandment? What immediate steps can be taken to strip them of their power?

4. Why is the first commandment essential to the foundation of solid faith community?

■▪

*You shall not make for yourself an idol
in the form anything in heaven above
or on the earth beneath or in the waters below.
You shall not bow down
to them or worship them. . . .*

2

Picture This!

An Unlimited God

I have never had another friend like my paternal grandfather, Jonathan Wade Marshall. We were the best of buddies and spent absurd amounts of time together when I was a child. He had one especially distinguishing characteristic. My grandfather would have made a great one-armed bandit. A piece of farm machinery ripped his right arm from his body and mangled it. For as long as I knew my grandfather, he was a one-armed man, possessing a complete left arm and a right nub that extended almost to elbow length.

By the time I began tagging along with him, Grandpa had adjusted quite well. As far as I could tell, that nub never seemed to handicap him. Occasionally we grandchildren could coax him into playing a game of baseball with us in the backyard. Grandpa would toss the ball in the air, grab and swing the bat with one arm, and still knock the ball further than any of us two-armed youngsters could hit it.

One of the most amazing things my one-armed grandfather did was drive his International pickup truck. That would not have been so memorable, except that the truck had a manual transmission. The gear shift lever was on the right side of the steering column—and my grandpa's good arm was the left one. I can still see him change gears: release the accelerator, depress the clutch, press his right nub of an arm against the steering wheel to steady it, reach through the steering wheel with his left arm, grab the gear shift, and change gears. It was an awesome feat to behold.

The point is that I had never known my grandfather to be anything other than a one-armed man, though that was never a negative or limiting condition in any way, as far as I could see. But that changed one Christmas when the Marshall clan gathered at my aunt's house for our holiday meal.

Hanging along the walls of the hallway were several pictures of Marshall ancestors. Virtually all of these were photographs that I had never seen. One picture, a family shot, caught my attention. In it, my oldest uncle and aunt were teenagers. My dad was a cute little pint-sized fellow in overalls. My grandparents had dark hair instead of white hair, as I had always known them to have. But something was puzzling about that picture.

As I studied it, I initially thought it was because everyone was younger. But suddenly I discovered another reason: my grandfather had two arms. He had one arm more than I had ever seen attached to his body. It was an eerie experience because the image portrayed in the picture did not match the reality I had known. After the tingles and light-headedness ceased, I was able to acknowledge how my grandfather looked at an earlier time in his life.

Pictures sometimes distort the truth. Other times they do not distort the truth, but instead present it from another perspective. During the time of Henry the VIII, so a story goes, an artist painted a portrait of a certain young woman. Although this woman possessed a natural beauty, acne or some other skin disorder scarred her face. As the artist worked on the portrait, however, he fell hopelessly in love with the woman. His finished product showed a smooth-skinned face, with radiant beauty to rival that of any woman in the area.

Henry VIII, prior to his poor track record with six other wives, saw the portrait and decided he had to have this woman for his wife—until he saw her in the flesh. The image portrayed in the painting did not match the reality of the flesh. Henry decided he could not marry her and instead gave her a job in the kitchen. Ironically enough, that likely prolonged her life, since Henry's six marriages did not have happy endings.

When asked why he had misrepresented her, the artist said he painted her as *he* saw her through the eyes of love. This is a tribute to the painter, but another example of how images do not always match reality.

Most of us know what this is like from looking at our own personal photographs. Some of us never imagined we could wear such stupid grins on our faces until we posed for a camera. We never realized we had red eyes that glow like hot embers, but that is the way the photograph represented us.

Sometimes it is a difference between what is real and what is represented. Other times the representation is accurate, while the misconception is in our understanding. But in either case, there is often a discrepancy between a photograph and a person, a gap between representation and reality, between image and individual.

These examples provide some direction for thinking about the second commandment's prohibition of idols: "You shall not make for yourself an idol in the form of anything in heaven or on earth beneath or in the waters be-

low. You shall not bow down to them or worship them."
The Israelites flirted with idols from time to time. Jacob
and Rachel's conflict with Laban in Genesis 31 includes a
dispute over possession of the teraphim—religious statues
or idols kept in the home. In Exodus 32, the Israelites grew ·
impatient waiting for Moses to come down off the mountain. They made a golden calf to worship as an idol, a visual representation of God.

Over the centuries, Israel's flirtation with idolatry was
bad enough that the prophet Isaiah took time in chapter 44
to poke fun at those who cut down a tree and made an
idolatrous representation of God from one end and fire-
wood from the other.[1] So the Israelites did have a problem
restraining themselves from creating idols which served as
visual representations of God.

If idols are simply visual representations of God, why
is there a prohibition against them? Might not their use
help to keep God foremost in our lives, as the first commandment requires? One reason for their prohibition is
that idols are never *just* a visual representation. They gradually become objects of allegiance and ultimately are hal-
lowed as holy relics of some sort.

If for instance, someone believes they have seen the
face of Jesus in leaves of a tree, at first it reminds people of
Jesus. Then, people flock to the tree, and it is decorated as
a shrine. Next, people bring gifts and offerings, not to
mention the sick and diseased, and lay them at the foot of
this decorated tree and expect the Jesus tree (by that point
Jesus and *tree* are blurred together in people's thinking) to
answer their prayers and dispense the requested favors.
So what started as a tree whose leaves reminded someone
of Jesus becomes an object of worship. Suddenly something other than God is receiving the loyalty and devotion
that the first command restricts to God alone.

As another example, think of the mind-set that accompanies voodoo dolls as portrayed in movies. The doll is a representation of the person, who supposedly can be controlled by acts performed on the doll. Sticking a pin into the doll is believed to cause pain to the person it represents. I have no direct knowledge of this religion; I am simply giving an example from popular culture.

This last example moves us a step further in understanding the prohibition against idols. The issue is partially one of containing and controlling God. An idol can be picked up or disregarded as one chooses. The idol, and supposedly God, can be used whenever desired, and thus is to some degree at the mercy and disposal of its owner.

To fashion an idol is to attempt to cut God down to size and to assume that God is susceptible to our control. It is to fall into a trap like the little boy who had been praying to God but could see no evidence that his prayers were being answered. In a final step of desperation, he went into the living room, took the statue of the virgin Mary off the mantle over the fireplace, and sneaked back to his room. With the statue firmly in his clutches, he wrote a letter that began, "Dear God: If you ever want to see your mother again . . ." Idols give people a sense of being able to control God.

Another reason idols are prohibited is more closely aligned with the stories of my grandfather's picture and the artist's painting. Picture this: you have the opportunity to make a replica of God, to create an image that expresses what and who God is. What would that image look like? How accurately would it portray the reality of God?

We get a glimpse of the problem when we pause to think of how Jesus is portrayed in paintings and literature. If Caucasians produce the painting, Jesus is white, usually with brown hair and blue eyes. If an African-American is responsible for the picture, Jesus is usually dark skinned. I have never seen an Asian portrait of Jesus, but I'd expect him to have slanted eyes. When we add to that practice the words of Colossians 1:15, which says that Jesus is the image of the invisible God—and we have made Jesus look like us—well, you can see how people could be deluded into thinking they have captured a representation of God.[2]

If we were to craft an idol intended to be nothing more than a visual representation of God, where would we begin? We would try to be true to what God is and to be inclusive. Yet the reality of God will match the image we create as badly as that two-armed man in the picture fitted the memory I have of my grandfather. There may be a lot of similarities, but it is not a perfect match. Therefore, misrepresentation occurs.

Israel and surrounding cultures were prone to represent their gods by means of the forces of nature and society that they recognized. So also, our ideas about God and the traits we ascribe to God are often based on our imperfect impressions, formed from what we experience in the world at large and consequently attribute to God. Those ideas and images are then used to interpret ideas and images of God contained in our sacred literature. But we do not know enough! God is too much for us ever to accurately portray through an image of any kind.

We cannot help but do some of that as we experience, think, and talk about God. The idolatry comes when we limit who God is, or what God can be, to our picture of the Divine. At that point we not only create a picture of God; we frame it. That frame sets boundaries within which God must act in order to be acknowledged by us.

So part of the problem is that idolatry denies God's magnificence and transcendence. An accompanying problem is thinking God could be accurately represented by something made from a motionless piece of wood, or a cold, hard stone. This also denies God's relational capacity. A piece of wood or stone, as far as we know, does not think, feel, rejoice, suffer, or experience—any of those things that God does in relation with creation, according to the Bible.

The prohibition against idols extends far beyond making statuesque forms. It is concerned with human attempts to control our Creator. It tries to discourage efforts to create a picture, an image, an *understanding* of God that not only frames and limits how we conceive God, but also seriously doubts that God could be anything else.

A modern application of this commandment does not require that we possess little statues. The Quaker author, Douglas Gwyn, suggests that contemporary idols are not graven images, but are ideals and ideologies. The word *idea* comes from the Greek *idein*, and the word *theory* is derived from *theōrein*, each of which means "to see."[3] Thus the connection is made between seeing and image, and hence idols. Gwyn is correct when he says some of us are prone to "serve our favorite ideas with the same scrupulous devotion that ancient idolaters gave to their graven images."[4]

This is true whether we are talking about the fundamentalist, liberal, or even centrist Christian beliefs. It is the case whether the picture of God is loving to the point of being domesticated, holy to the point of being unapproachable, or so inclusive that a definite decision about God can never be reached. It is especially true when we are rigidly locked into our assumptions and expectations of what God can and cannot do, for consequently, we deny God's power and sovereignty.

We move from ancient practice to contemporary relevance by asking ourselves, "Is our picture or our mental image of God so framed and defined that *we* have decided what God is and is not? Have we determined what the Lord likes and dislikes, will do and will not do, to the point that we have ruled out all other possibilities? Do we have any idolatrous representations, perhaps physical, perhaps mental, by which we would limit the power and movement of God among us?" This is not to say that we could prevent God from being anything else, only that we would refuse to acknowledge it.

Negatively stated, the second commandment says we shall not fashion God's likeness after anything we know, because there is so much surrounding who God is that we can never completely and sufficiently represent God. God cannot be restricted to an image, a shrine, or a territory. Positively stated, after the first commandment's insistence that we serve one God alone, this commandment says there is no limit to who God is and what God can do. To love and serve God, we must know God. To know God, we must experience the Divine Presence and Power freely and with an open mind.

The solution to worshiping God without an image is found in a theology of God's presence. We must know God in reality, not in form. We must learn to recognize God in our experience, not from a statue. We must identify God according to the Divine words and deeds, not from visual representations. The Bible calls people to listen to God and recognize what God does rather than to try to see God (Exod. 33:20).

The first commandment says our ultimate commitment must be to God. The second says, believing that, we must be open for anything to happen. Imagine this, if you will: a God for whom no picture can do justice, but who in the context of the covenant relationship and through the Divine Presence, will always be showing us something wonderful, real, and perhaps new. What a picture!

■▪

There is no limit to who God is and what God can do.

For Discussion

1. Think about your conception of God. Are there any obvious stereotypes that need to be confronted and dismissed, such as a mental image of an old man with a long white beard?

2. What are the dangers of idolatrous representations of God? How are they not limited only to statues?

3. Can you name ways that we attempt to control our Creator and justify our own plans through the way we represent God's desires?

4. Name at least two ways you can begin to trust God's unlimited possibilities.

■▪

*You shall not misuse the name of
the Lord your God, for the Lord
will not hold anyone guiltless
who misuses his name.*

3

Name It and Claim It!

Misrepresenting the Divine Agenda

Before FM radio was popular and stereo systems enhanced reception quality, radio listeners in Siler City, North Carolina, were at the mercy of the only AM station in town: WNCA, 1610 on the radio dial. Local residents could receive the signals of a few other stations, but WNCA was the sole local option.

Radio stations have long used gimmicks designed to encourage listeners in radio land to tune to their frequency. WNCA was no exception. Their attraction was a game called "Name It and Claim It!" With only a moment's notice, the disc jockey invited listeners to call in while a record was being played. The tenth caller was given the opportunity to name the title of the song. Give the name, and claim the prize. For correct identification, the participant could claim a 28-ounce nonreturnable bottle of Pepsi Cola. How lucky can you get?

Another game, played by a station whose call letters I do not remember, changed the rules a bit. Instead of taking calls from the listeners, the radio officials selected a random phone number, dialed it, and allowed the phone to ring six times. If someone answered, the disk jockey introduced himself and asked a question. Of course, if the question was answered properly, the person called could claim the prize.

How often I heard that game being played when I was a child! I wanted them to call me so badly I could hardly stand it. Sometimes I would actually pray, "Lord, please let them call me." I would promise to share my reward, my windfall profits, with the church.

One Saturday afternoon our phone rang, and I answered. The person calling identified himself as someone with WNCA. Although I didn't recognize his name, I knew those call letters. He said our number had been selected to play "Name It and Claim It!"

"Is this 742-3885?" he asked.

"Yes it is," I stammered, hardly able to contain myself.

"What is your name?"

"Jay Marshall," I answered clearly.

"And how old are you?" the disk jockey questioned. . . . "Ten? Well, that's old enough to play our game. Here's your question: What was the Lone Ranger's horse's name?"

Well, I knew the answer to that. Who didn't? In that barren, pre-cable TV wilderness, we only had three TV stations, four if the weather was clear. So if a person watched television at all, chances were they had seen the Masked Man ride his faithful steed and were familiar with his trademark: "Hi ho, Silver."

I swallowed really hard, trying to calm my nerves and steady my voice: "The answer is Silver."

"Are you sure?"

"Yes sir. I'm positive!" I replied confidently, and the adrenaline began to surge through my body, pulsating even to the tips of my toes.

In an excited voice, the disk jockey shouted, "You're absolutely right! And for that correct answer, you win today's grand prize. Do you know what that is today, Jay Marshall?"

"No-o-o," I replied, although dollar signs were dancing in my mind, because that was the normal prize.

The voice on the other end of the phone said, "As our grand prize winner for correctly naming the Lone Ranger's horse, we're going to send you the biggest bucket of fresh horse manure you've ever seen. Will that make you happy, Jay Marshall? Now, what is your address?"

I hung up and spent the rest of the day worrying about what I was going to do if they discovered my address and that rank package arrived. I had named the correct name and was now expected to claim a prize I would never have requested in my wildest ten-year-old dreams.

On Monday morning, I discovered that WNCA had not called at all. Instead, it was a new kid in school who was desperate for attention. For the next few days, I made sure he received it!

Name the name, and lay claim to the prize. The "name it and claim it" concept intersects with the third commandment. In the game, as a reward for knowing the proper name, the winner was given the authority to make a certain claim and could expect certain things, whether it was Pepsi or organic fertilizer. In ancient Israel, naming the name of Yahweh created similar expectations.

Personal names were important in Israel. They had meanings in and of themselves. They were often theophoric names, in which the divine name joined with a noun or verb produced a sentence name. For example, *Jonathan* is *ya* (abbreviated form of *Yahweh, Lord*) and *nathan* (to give); thus it means "the Lord has given." *Elijah* is *eli* (my God) and *ya* (Lord); it means "the Lord is my God." Parents often chose a name for their child in hopes that it would express the child's personality in adulthood. Of course, that makes one wonder what the parents were thinking when they named their child "Gareb," which means "Scabby"; or "Nabal," which means "Fool." Parents have their reasons, I suppose.

The Israelites considered names to be powerful. To know someone's name was to know the person as well as something about that person, since the name expressed the essence of the personality. Knowing the name supposedly gave a person power over the other one whose name was known, as when the first man named the animals (Gen. 2:19-20). This is symbolized in certain name-destroying rituals designed to symbolically eliminate the enemy. Using someone's name implied that some of their power and prestige came to the user. To name the name was to claim at least some of the authority that accompanied it.

That idea is not completely foreign to us. Name dropping, letters of reference by someone with a prominent name, and co-signing promissory notes—these perform similar functions. Certain names open doors and gain privileges. To possess the name is to have access to some of the power that accompanies it. It allows us to be privy to the character and influence of that name.

With that background information, what kind of doors would the name of God open? Consider what God was actually revealing in the burning bush episode (Exod. 3). When God commissioned Moses to lead the Israelites out of Egypt, Moses protested on the grounds that he did not know God's name. That is to say, Moses did not know God's nature or character. Furthermore, he did not know how to summon God when he needed God's help. God solved that dilemma, instructing Moses, "Tell the Israelites that Yahweh sent you."

The name Yahweh means "I am" or "I will be" or "I will

cause to be," depending on how one translates it. "I am who I am," or "I will be who I will be," or "I will cause to be what I will cause to be." When God said to Moses, "My name is I AM," in effect, God was saying, "I can be whatever I choose to be and I can be whatever a deity needs to be in order for you to be the leader I am calling you to be."

I think God told Moses and the Israelites just enough to whet their appetites. When God said, "My name is I AM," the natural response is to ask, "You are who, or what?" At that point, the Israelites, and we, all become theologians. Who do you think God is? What do you think God is like? To answer that question, we try to describe with what God would be associated, and what things God endorses. The name "I AM" reveals something about God's personality and the freedom that accompanies it; but beyond that, it does not give many specifics.

God helped the Israelites figure out some of the implications of "I am" at the beginning of the Ten Commandments. At the outset of the covenant, God was saying, "I AM the Lord your God, and I AM the one who brought you out of Egypt." From that, the Israelites were assured that God worked for them not against them, was gracious toward them rather than hostile, and that God was a revealing, relational deity rather than detached and remote.

Over the centuries, the biblical writers gave some 700 names for God. These names illuminate how people experienced and interpreted the Divine nature and identity. For instance, Yahweh Sabbaoth—Lord of Hosts; El Shaddai—God Almighty; El Roi—The God Who Sees. Such names help describe who I AM really is.

God did a courageous thing in revealing the divine name. Once one's name is known, a person can be represented—or misrepresented—by any who know the name. They can name the name and then lay claim to whatever the "prize" is at the moment. This is easily observable in even the most routine events. "Mother said, 'Let me play with that toy,' " carries more weight than "I want to play with that toy." "The boss wants me to do this job; you take that one" has more authority than "let me do that job." The right name in front of the claim brings results. That is the key to understanding the third commandment.

Older translations read, "Thou shalt not take the name of the Lord in vain" (KJV). Recent versions help us understand: "You shall not misuse the name of God" (NIV). Members of the faith community must be careful not to misrepresent God and make claims in God's name that are, in fact, false.

What does it mean to misuse the name of the Lord? For as long as I can remember, I was taught that the essence of this commandment was concerned with profanity, specifically placing the word *God* in front of a commonly known four-letter word whose homonym is a water barrier. Other four-letter words were frowned upon by my teachers and elders, but this one was especially sinful because it took God's name in vain. Through that distinction, we learned a hierarchy of profanity, which was clearly a terrible trivialization of the third commandment!

In the Bible, cursing is the opposite of blessing. *Blessing* conveys wishes and helps bring the abundance of God's presence and provision into a person's or community's life. *Cursing* is the opposite—denying or attempting to withhold or cut off those blessings from another person. The only connection between the big *G* curse words and the third commandment is that as a subject and verb, it invokes God to curse or to withhold from another person (James 3:9-10). In effect, it asks God to destroy that person's future. None of us can claim the right to instruct God to act in that way.

Negatively stated, the commandment means: Do not misuse the name of the Lord in order to make claims we think are worthy. Do not "name it" in order to "claim it." Beware of using the name of God in order to justify claiming something to which we are not otherwise entitled. Positively stated, claim that God endorses only things you are certain God endorses. Let us not claim that God is for doing what we are for doing, unless we have spent so much time in prayer and soul-searching that we are confident God's will does lead us in that direction. In short, this command tells us not to use God's name, the divine credentials, to validate or bathe our desires in religious authority, or to perpetuate agendas that are not in harmony with who God is and what God is about.

Despite the presence of this command in the Decalogue, occasionally the prophets lamented that this very thing was occurring. They noted how corruption in Israelite society was combined with claims that "surely the Spirit of God is among us." There are numerous places where similar claims are being made today. "Holy wars" wage violent aggression in the name of God; they are a misuse of God's name. People seek to justify such actions by having them sanctioned by the deity.

In Jesus' day, people were quite casual about using the Lord's name to reinforce their words, vows, and goals. In the Sermon on the Mount, Jesus instructed his followers, "Do not swear at all." Do not try to manipulate God to serve your own purposes. Instead, "Simply let your 'Yes' be 'Yes,' and your 'No,' 'No'; anything beyond this comes from the evil one" (Matt. 5:33-37).

There are other examples of misusing God's name that occur in everyday conversation. Twelve years ago I had the pleasure of knowing and worshiping with some charismatic Christians. I learned many things from them, positively and negatively. A negative one came from listening to the manner in which one particular woman thought and taught about using the name of God and Jesus. To ask for something in their name—to "name it," so to speak—was to "claim it," or insure that God would grant the request, if one had enough faith. She quoted John 14:14, "If you ask anything in my name, I will do it" (KJV).[1] That can be a dangerous claim, if we do not understand what it means to ask in Jesus' name.

On one occasion she shared with the group that she had recently been praying for a new car. The one car she wanted more than any other was a bright, new Mercedes. Because God had to give her anything she asked for in the name of Jesus (it was scriptural), she had been praying for a Mercedes in Jesus' name. She wanted us to know what temptations that could bring; just that day she had seen a beautiful Mercedes. She was about to decide that was the specific car she was to pray for, and then she realized Satan had been tempting her. This was a maroon Mercedes, and she specifically had asked God for a blue one! Is this an appropriate use of the name of God? No. Instead it illustrates the third commandment's meaning when it says, "Do not misuse the name of God."

This story is not intended as a statement against the charismatic faith. Her faith was sincere. The problem was that she did not understand what it meant to pray and ask "in the name of Jesus." It means to pray in the character or the manner in which Jesus would pray. It does not mean prayer is a rubber stamp that forces God to grant our every wish simply because we said the magic words.

Similar assumptions often pervade our descriptions of God's actions on our behalf. I heard once of a town that was in the path of a hurricane. The townspeople prayed that God would divert the hurricane and save them. As requested, the hurricane turned away and charted a different course. The town was saved!

However, on this new course, the hurricane wrecked another town a few miles northeast. The loss of life and property was significant. As the people in the spared town rejoiced over what God had done, we wonder what the people in the other town thought about God at that moment. The people in the town that escaped destruction had named the name and claimed the prize. But was God responsible for turning the hurricane away? If so, was God responsible for the lives and property in the other town as well?

Sincere believers often counter such questions by appealing to our lack of knowledge of God's ways and will. Certainly we cannot completely know the mind and heart of God. But it is also possible that the claims we make about God's actions represent our desires to be protected by God more than they accurately represent God. The third command teaches that when we use the name of God, we need to be mindful of the implications those claims make. We are not only making statements about what we believe; we are also making claims for who and what God is.

The "name it and claim it" principle can strike even closer home for us. Perhaps more relevant to our situation is taking the name *Christian* as we claim to be children of God, but carelessly living, thinking, and acting in ways that do not honor that name. If that is our case, we name the name and claim the grace, but use grace to erase the implications and responsibilities of unchristian behavior.

We might think of people who wear a golden cross around their necks or on their lapels, but never consider emulating the sacrifice to which it witnesses. In that case, do we misuse the symbol and the name associated with it to make false claims about ourselves?

When we join a church congregation and receive membership, we agree to uphold the ministry for God's kingdom in our prayers, presence, and gifts. But if we then renege on that covenant and disappear from the life of the church, we are violating the third commandment. For reasons such as these, Jesus said, "Not everyone who says to me, 'Lord, Lord,' will enter the kingdom of heaven" (Matt. 7:21). One might call on the name but make false claims. Within the covenant community, it is crucial that we seek to know and promote the purposes of the one who called us, rather than to use that name to further purely personal agendas. As we name the name and claim the prize of divine grace, we enter the community of faith. Now our purposes must extend far beyond using the name of the Lord to get a Mercedes, divert a hurricane, or even win a bucket of horse manure. The third commandment reminds us that living in faithful relationship with God includes credible representation of our Creator on this earth.

■■

Learn to distinguish between
God's desires and human wants.

For Discussion

1. How were names important in ancient Israel? What was the significance of God revealing the divine name to Moses?

2. What are the dangers of capriciously giving God credit for things that may not be a direct result of God's intervention?

3. What are some ways that God's name is misused in society? by the church? by you?

■▪

*Remember the Sabbath and keep
it holy. Six days you shall labor
and do all your work, but the
seventh day is a Sabbath day
to the Lord your God.*

4

R. I. P.

Rest for the Soul

When it comes to rest, one man set a record, according to legend. His name is familiar to you: Rip Van Winkle. He was a happy mortal with a strong aversion to work. Rip took the world easy, ate white bread or brown, whichever could be had with the least thought or trouble, and would rather starve on a penny than work for a pound.

Rip Van Winkle would have gladly whistled life away in perfect idle contentment except that his wife's sharp tongue about his lazy ways droned in his ears night and day. To escape this henpecking, Rip Van Winkle would take his musket and dog to the Catskill Mountains to hunt squirrels and just generally relax upon a rock. On one of his outings, Rip happened upon a rugged-looking fellow carrying a keg up a steep ravine. After helping the man, Rip was offered a mug of this strange liquid.

The next thing Rip knew, he was waking from a deep sleep. Thinking he had spent the night on a mountain, Rip returned to the village to find everything had changed . . .

for it was twenty years later. His friends were gone, his wife had died, his house had crumbled, his dog did not recognize him, and his young daughter was now grown, with a little child of her own.[1]

That must have been some nap for Rip Van Winkle! This man, whom everyone presumed dead, was really only resting peacefully upon the mountain. R. I. P. could have identified his grave and served as an appropriate epitaph. But what a rude shock when he awakened and returned home. The story of Rip Van Winkle is only a fairy tale. Nevertheless, it can teach us as we study the meaning of the fourth commandment with its admonition to keep the Sabbath holy and to rest in peace.

As I use the acronym of R. I. P., it does refer to *rest in peace*. It is not, however, used as a wish for those who are dead. Instead, it is an invitation that, if accepted, is designed to keep us out of the spiritual grave.

In our daily lives, we encounter several places that tell us to "rest." There are spaces called "rest rooms," which seems like a strange name for such places since we really do not rest there. There are "restaurants," another oddly named place, where one may rest and replenish physical needs. More appropriately named are "rest stops," which are welcome additions to the nation's bustling roadways.

Other types of rest include commas and periods in sentences. These tell us when to rest while speaking or reading. When observed, they add order, nuance, and meaning to our language. Musical rests slow or halt the musician, and in the process enhance the rhythm and character of the musical piece.

For our enjoyment, there are designated periods of rest called vacations. While they provide a welcome break from our normal routines, vacations seldom leave us rested. That is because we often stuff such a multitude of work, hobbies, trips, and tours into our rest period that we are dragging with fatigue by the time the vacation is over.

The most common and frequently practiced type of rest is the peace we enter each night called sleep. But not all sleep is restful or peaceful, as people who suffer from nightmares or insomnia will attest. Other behavior is not as dramatic as nightmares but yet fairly annoying to others in the room. Some people, in a restless state of sleep, carry on wild and vivid conversations or do other strange things. One night I was awakened by four musical clear notes as my wife, Judi, sang "A-mer-i-ca." That's it. Only one word—just enough to wake me and cause me to wonder if she was having patriotic dreams. I have no excuse to talk, though, since she says I tend to laugh in my sleep.

Rest, when we get it, seems temporarily to slow activity and in the process add to the quality of the activity, whether it is travel, language, music, or our bodies and minds. Those analogies help us begin to appreciate the spirit of the Sabbath regulation, which reminded Israel's covenant community of their need to rest.

The word Sabbath comes from the Hebrew *shabbat*, which means rest. So we could read the commandment "Remember the Rest-day by keeping it holy. Six days you shall labor and do all your work, but the seventh day is a Rest-day to the Lord your God." The Exodus version of the Ten Commandments bases this commandment on the fact that God also rests. According to the Genesis creation story, after creating everything from sunlight to gnats, including the gift of human life, God rested (Gen. 2:3). This act of divine rest became the theological framework for the Sabbath regulation.

The Sabbath became a special day set aside to remind the Israelites that the cycle of life should include a period of rest, refreshment, *and* remembering their Creator. When Israel remembered their Creator, they remembered that this was the One who also had delivered them from bondage. When they remembered that newly acquired freedom, they remembered the covenant.

Thus it is no surprise that when we read Deuteronomy's version of the Decalogue in chapter five, the reason given for observing the Sabbath is not because God rested, but because God brought them out of Egypt. What we begin to see is that the Sabbath-rest was about more than relaxation from toil and labor. It was about more than rejuvenation of tired muscles and aching backs. The Sabbath became a weekly reminder for the Jews of the Passover, and what God had done to create this covenant community. In a similar way, Sunday should remind Christians of Easter, the resurrection faith, and our place in the faith community where we serve our Lord.

Over time, moralists, legalists, as well as good intentioned elders and rabbis, elaborately interpreted the spirit of the regulation. Consequently, what began as a healthy command became cluttered with excessive obligations and tedious definitions. How far could one walk on the Sabbath without it being considered work? Where should the blessing be given during the Sabbath meal—before or after the wine? Rules were multiplied until, seemingly, it would have been more tiring to keep the Sabbath than to just forfeit the idea of a day of rest. The Sabbath became an opportunity for the people to show what they were willing to do for God. This displaced the focus on remembering God's deliverance and gracious gift of covenant to the people, and celebrating the covenant relationship,

The spirit of the law of Sabbath-rest is about remembering that life has purpose and meaning which transcend our efforts to provide the basic necessities and to get ahead in life. Keeping the Sabbath holy involves drawing near to the Lord of our covenant and desiring that sweet communion of fellowship. There is more behind this command than a desire for a periodic breather. The Sabbath regulation has a way of calming our gnawing anxieties to be in control, to get ahead and stay there, or to always be busy. Those anxieties make us so intent to take care of ourselves that we are actually prone to disregard our needs physically, emotionally, and spiritually.

Judi and I spent part of a recent vacation in the Bahamas. If you have never been there, you need to understand that tourism is the breath of life in their economy. They have done a fine job catering to those of us who wish to enjoy their island paradise. Our final day there was a Sunday, and our ship was to depart at 4:30 p.m. So naturally, we were hoping to see and do as many things as possible right up to the last moment. But we discovered the most remarkable thing. Almost everything closes on Sunday: the bus system that shuttles tourists; the straw market, which sells Bahamian-made wares; the shops at the international market; the snorkeling and parasailing—everything, except the casinos. We were stunned.

There were thousands of tourists there on Sunday. Together they represented hundreds of thousands of dollars, which translates into profitable opportunities for the people of the island. Nevertheless, on Saturday evening they turned their backs on the money, closed their shops, and went home. Instead of business, they chose rest and family and play, and many of them chose church. It seemed like a novel idea except for the fact that God has been telling people this all along. The Sabbath command asks us to step away from the frantic pace of the routine and step into the holiness of God's presence so that we may rest in God's peace.

Let us recognize how out of sync we are with the Sabbath-rest. All we have to do is observe the difficulty we have maintaining a Sabbath rhythm that values rest, communion, and relationships more than busyness, profit, and self-advancement. One of our biggest problems in that respect is that we have lost a sense of the holiness of the Sabbath. Holiness has slipped between the cracks, so that the idea of rest stands alone. The ways by which we are eager to rest are often not sacred but secular, and sometimes profane. It is easy to forsake holy rest for the pursuit of our jobs and the success of our professions. We might be attracted by the pervasive, crass materialism that is squeezing us into the world's mold (Rom. 12:2). This hinders us from settling in the restful presence of the One who decided to create us in the Divine image. In our society, it is far more common to find people who are driven by their passions than those who prefer to rest in and be empowered by God's presence. In fact, sometimes we are more prone to evade God's presence than to seek it.

Think of what it is like when we decide to invite guests to our homes. Sometimes in our determination to be good hosts, we hustle about making sure that everyone has silverware, or all the beverage glasses are filled, or the thermostat is turned low enough to maintain a comfortable level. While trying to be such good hosts, we can easily ignore the guests and not enjoy their company.

When we keep the Sabbath holy, we do not rest alone. We are joined by a holy Guest, whose presence is vital if we are to rest in peace. Without attending to that presence, without maintaining the connection between holy and rest, our leisure is more akin to that of Rip Van Winkle. We idly pass the time until one day we are startled by the fact that nothing in our life is as we remember it. We will have dug a spiritual grave that offers little peace.

As a covenant people, if we wish to honor the Sabbath, we must begin by rejoining holy with rest. We must recognize that the Sabbath is not designed so much to promote inactivity as it is a sign of our activity as dependents. The Sabbath teaches us to rest and wait upon God, to relish lounging in the divine presence, and to let our actions arise out of the inner promptings God gives us during those times. In addition to relaxation, it is rejuvenation. More than going on vacation, Sabbath-rest resorts to meditation. More than overcoming weariness, it provides us with spiritual direction.

In grammar, we learn of the active voice, showing that we take action. There is also the passive voice, which is when we are acted upon. But there is also a middle voice, in which we both act and are acted upon. We participate in the formation of action and reap the benefits of it. As Eugene Peterson describes it, "We neither manipulate God (active voice) or are manipulated by God (passive voice). We are involved in the action and participate in its results but do not control or define it (middle voice).[2]

Peterson's point is helpful for thinking about the Sabbath-rest. We do not observe the Sabbath to please God (active) so that God will in turn be good to us (passive). We observe the Sabbath to commune with our Creator. We remember our relationship with God. We recall our identity as children of God. Through these acts of remembering, we become grateful for those things. In that state of mindfulness we become more aware of the presence of God.

From that middle state of giving and receiving, we emerge more than refreshed. We also emerge inspired, directed, and focused, more firmly convinced of God's communion in our lives and of our place in God's community than ever before. Through our participation in this rest, we give room for God to prepare and assist us in the keeping of the covenant commands.

In Richard Foster's book, *Prayer*,[3] he suggests three things to help us learn to rest the Sabbath-rest: *solitude*, by which he means some time spent apart from our normal routines; *silence*, in which we are centered in God's presence; and *recollection*, a remembrance which he believes helps us focus on the moment. I suspect those three things help us know where we have been and where we are in our spiritual journey. They help us receive the peace and direction God would give us in those restful moments. God said to the covenant community, "Remember the Rest-day and keep it holy." Later, Jesus taught that we were not made for the Sabbath, but that the Sabbath was made for us (Mark 2:27-28). That means observing the Sabbath-rest is related to our well-being as much as anything else. In our busy world with its seemingly impossible demands, I am hopeful that what the writer of Hebrews told his congregation is true for us as well: "a sabbath rest still remains for the people of God" (4:9). It is the day of salvation. This means rest now for believers, as they regularly gather to worship God, encourage each other, and anticipate their coming inheritance (10:25); and a future fulfillment of rest in God's presence.[4]

So the hope expressed in the fourth commandment for us as individuals and as members of a faith community covenanted with God is that we may learn to rest in peace. Not in the fashion of the tombstone—at least not yet. Not the escapist, irresponsible sleep of Rip Van Winkle. Not the restless tossing and turning of a spiritual insomniac. The hope is that we will all rest a Sabbath-rest, which like any good rest, be it musical or otherwise, can only enhance the meaning and rhythm within our life of faith. Rest in Peace, my friends.

■

Relax frequently in the divine presence, and let God rejuvenate your life.

For Discussion

1. How did observance of the Sabbath-rest help Israel to keep the covenant?

2. Does our observance of Sunday as a Christian equivalent to the Sabbath accomplish the purposes of the fourth commandment?

3. Thinking of the Sabbath-rest as "middle voice," what are some of the ways you can help reconnect "holy" with "rest"?

4. We all know that many secular options discourage the Sabbath-rest. How about our faith community? Do its activities encourage rest and rejuvenation?

■◻

*Honor your father and your
mother, so that you may live long
in the land the Lord your God is giving you.*

5

Get Real!

*Basing Relationships on Honesty
and Integrity*

One double-dipped ice-cream cone. A total cost of $1.98. It does not sound like much, but it was a gift that really made one young man's day.

Some friends of mine recently returned from a vacation. One afternoon, after much walking and sightseeing, they spied a little ice-cream shop tucked in a corner of a strip mall. Their taste buds took a vote, and a unanimous count convinced them the shop was a must-see attraction.

As they placed their order at the counter, they noticed a young man, probably in his early twenties, whose physical features suggested that he was mentally and socially challenged. He stood quietly near the counter, eyes glued to the many flavors of frozen treats. He shook his head no when the woman working the counter asked if she could help him.

My friends took their ice cream and found a table for two near the window. Even as their taste buds applauded the first bite, they became aware that this young man had come to stand by their table. As soon as eye contact was made, the young man asked, "Will you buy me an ice cream cone?"

My friends are not ones to waste money, and giving cash to strangers never makes their list of "things to do today." But for some reason, this seemed like an appropriate gesture. Giving away two dollars would not ruin their day. As one of them reached into his pocket for the two bucks, a young fellow across the room said, "Hey, I'll go in halves with you on this," and handed over a dollar of his own.

With some help from the store clerk, the young man chose strawberry ice cream and paid for his purchase. He returned one cent to each of the donors, uttered a polite thank you, and exited the building. Only after he was gone did the store clerk comment on the situation. She came out to the table where my friends sat and said, "Thank you for what you just did. That was the sixth time this guy has been in our store today. You are the first to acknowledge his presence and honor his request. I think you've made his day. He feels a little more like a real person now."

It is sad that we humans are sometimes oblivious to the needs of others around us, even if they are standing before us where they can easily be seen. It is especially lamentable if our ignoring of others makes them feel abnormal, unacceptable, or less than human, simply because they make us uncomfortable in some way. No matter how challenged an individual may be, we all like to feel as though we are real.

Becoming real is a theme in a well-known children's story titled *The Velveteen Rabbit*.[1] Perhaps you know the story. The Velveteen Rabbit was a stuffed toy given as a Christmas gift to a little boy. But with all the new presents, the Velveteen Rabbit was soon forgotten, and eventually began to think he was worthless.

As the story unfolds, through a conversation with another discarded toy, the Skin Horse, the Velveteen Rabbit learned that being real and valuable has little to do with how one is made, but with whether or not one is loved. Although this is a children's story, it is also more than that. It articulates the human desire to be loved and accepted. The story is about growing old gracefully. And if we are fortunate, it is a parable about an attitude that we develop over the course of our lives.

People desire to be loved and accepted from the day we enter this world. As we grow through childhood into adolescence, people who care about us help us to know we are loved and accepted. They may even pamper us along the way. But once we become adults, the world expects us to have outgrown the need for affirmation. Society expects us to know who we are, and to have a sense of our own self-worth.

If life is partially about becoming real, the implication is that by adulthood, we are supposed to have arrived. Of course, I do not have to tell you that things are not always the way they are supposed to be or assumed to be. Sometimes we are not sure we are lovable or acceptable in our own eyes and the eyes of others. Worst of all, sometimes we are not even sure that God loves us. Consequently, it becomes extremely easy to deny love and acceptance to other people who need them as much as we do. If we do not feel real, we do not help others feel that way either.

The ice-cream shop incident and the story of the Velveteen Rabbit each make a statement about "getting real" through qualities such as recognition, affirmation, love, and acceptance. They also raise two important questions: How do we determine a person's value? And when, if ever, does someone become valueless? Perhaps those seem like strange or unimportant or even sacrilegious questions for us to ponder. Maybe we would even say that it is not our place to make such value judgments. The truth, however, is that rightly or wrongly, consciously or unconsciously, those valuations *are* made by our attitudes, our actions or inactions, and our policies toward and about people. That is precisely the concern of this fifth commandment as it applies to a specific topic.

The fifth command calls for people to honor their fathers and mothers. This command is not the only law regarding the treatment of parents. Following the Ten Commandments, the case law says, "Whoever strikes father or mother shall be put to death. . . . Whoever curses father or mother shall be put to death" (Exod. 21:15, 17, NRSV). If you are looking for harsh laws whose penalty appears extreme, look no further!

The character of these three commands is best understood by considering their verbs. The verb for "strike" (21:15) is *nakah*, which is more than an isolated strike or blow. It is an outright attack (as in NIV) on another person. The word "curse" (21:17) is from *qillel*, formed from a verb whose root meaning is to treat lightly or with contempt—to regard as of little account or no value. Cursing one's parents is not a matter of profanity but an issue of treating them with indignity. Honor (20:12), which is a translation of *kabod*, also means glory, and interestingly enough, weightiness. To honor someone in this Israelite context was to regard them as a person of worth and value—to acknowledge them as real, worthy of love and acceptance.

This command has traditionally been a parent's refuge when young children misbehave. However, the verse was probably not directed to young children at all, but to mature adults and the way they treated their aging parents. These commands were not designed initially as catechisms for young children. Instead, they were guidelines for founding a covenant community composed of family units united in a tribal federation.

These families were in the process of moving from Egyptian slavery, through a wilderness wandering, to the Promised Land. They were going from a setting where their Egyptian owners determined what they were given, and thus had some responsibility for their care; to a wilderness setting where the story says God provided for them; and eventually on to Canaan, the Promised Land. Once settled there, each clan received a land inheritance, and from that point on, each extended family had the primary responsibility of caring for their own.

To get a sense of the situation, picture yourself and family moving to a new, undeveloped area. Forget highways, fast food, and strip malls. You are settling so deep in the woods that sunshine barely filters through the forest canopy. Land must be cleared. There are crops to plant and tend. Herds of cattle and goats provide milk and meat, and you must raise and tend those herds. Besides this eternal list of chores, homes must be built and established.

In a situation like that, a family often struggles to feed mouths, clothe bodies, and make ends meet, but can hardly manage. When that is the case, people ask an uncomfortable question: "Who is expendable?" The answer is probably *not* the children, who have most of their lives before them, and whose young, energetic, virile bodies will soon help relieve the nearly insurmountable workload. They are needed to keep the family line going. The answer to the question "Who is expendable?" would probably be found on the other end of the age spectrum.

To combat that possibility, this commandment insisted that families honor the elderly, who were sometimes weaker and needier than their adult children. This law was designed to protect those who may be regarded as unimportant, unproductive, or burdensome.

Lest you think that is just an irrelevant concern in our twentieth-century setting, consider these statistics: half the world's people, nearly two and half billion, live in countries where the annual per capita income is $400 or less. At least 800 million people in those countries live in absolute poverty, beneath a rational definition of human decency. Nearly half a billion are chronically hungry, despite abundant harvests worldwide.[2] With numbers like that, we are tempted to think that everyone must fend for oneself just to survive. Can you imagine how tempting it must be to disregard those people who can no longer care for themselves and who offer ever-diminishing contributions to the family's survival?

Since most of us who reside in North America fall outside those categories, an example closer to home may sufficiently grab our attention. Reports of "senior abuse" continue to rise at an alarming rate. Some family members simply cannot cope with becoming a parent to their parent. Some lack the communication skills to discuss and defuse potentially abusive situations. The mounting frustration eventually helps trigger the physical and emotional assault of the most aged members of our population. Unless some remedy is found, this problem will become more pressing as life spans continue to lengthen in this age of medicine and technology, especially when life remains but quality of life does not.

Or think about this command from another angle. Imagine that when we reached the legal age of adulthood, our families and society did not consider us "free" or "independent." Rather than move out of our parents' domain and establish our own separate household, we remained subject to their ultimate authority. This was the scenario in Israel's tribal setting.

Imagine reaching twenty, thirty, or even forty years

old. By that time, you even have a family of your own, but your life is still almost completely regulated by the patriarch or matriarch of the family. He or she makes binding decisions for the whole family, including you and your children. How long do you suppose it would take for you to reach your boiling point? Once tempers reach a hard boil, we usually become bitter and angry. Dislike bordering on hatred grows until we are ready to lash out at every incident. We may seek ways to gain the upper hand in this situation.

At that point, those value judgments mentioned earlier regarding "who is worth what?" and "whose word counts?" and "who is expendable?" are being formulated. Once a negative verdict is rendered against a person's worth, it discards honor, dignity, and love and replaces them with spite and contempt. Suddenly, honoring the parent, the elderly, or any other person is not an easy accomplishment.

When we consider the context in which the command was given, it is clear that its motive is the preservation of family health and well-being as much, if not more, than holding parents in high regard. Regarding the human family, Frederick Buechner says, "It is not so much that things happen in a family as it is that the family is the things that happen in it. The family is continually becoming what becomes of it. It is every christening and every commencement, every falling in love, every fight, every departure, every return. A family is a web so delicately woven that it takes almost nothing to set the whole thing shuddering or even to tear it to pieces. Yet the thread it's woven of is as strong as anything on earth.[3]

Families *are* the building blocks of a community. Our lives are elaborately and inescapably linked. Just as it is true that what happens to a family is what a family becomes, so also that is true about the faith community. If

what happens in the lives of family and community is dis-
honoring, attacking, and disregarding people—whether
old or young, productive or not—that is what the community becomes. That is not what God desires in the covenant faith community, and indeed not for the world.

Israel was in a stressful situation of families trying to
grow and mature. The fledgling community was attempting to settle, unite, and prosper. In the midst of such a
situation, God gave this commandment to ensure that the
Israelite people remembered to get real and stay real. They
were to build genuine and authentic relationships based
on love and acceptance, even if at times it would be convenient to ignore or exclude certain groups such as their elders.

Many parents have a difficult time to keep from trying
to run their adult children's affairs. Dysfunctions in family
systems do not magically disappear once an adult child
leaves the nest. Hence, we may not be so far removed from
similar explosive attitudes and emotional scars. Consequently, contemporary faith communities need a commandment such as this one.

Perhaps the most valuable lesson to learn is not that
rote allegiance is due to someone because of biological relationship. The most important lesson is that in the faith
community, God has assigned infinite value to each person. Once God declares a person is real, made in his image
(Gen. 1:27), that one can never become unreal. And so
long as they are real, they deserve honor and integrity,
love and acceptance, each of which is a benefit of the fifth
commandment. Thus, the qualities upheld by this commandment become integral keys to healthy relationships
and faithful communities.

As for the implementation of these values, unfortu-
nately this commandment provides no specific guidelines.
The commandment says, "Just do it." Perhaps that allows

us to construe it as open-ended in terms of method. Any way that honors people is appropriate, though giving life to that honor may require some thought on our part. Jesus called for people to "help" father and mother, with no dodges and excuses allowed (Matt. 15:3-9). No doubt, the logical starting point is for us to produce simple and practical expressions of honoring, loving, visiting, and accepting others. We each have to figure out what that means for us personally, but we can gain counsel from our church community or sharing group.

So when it comes to honoring parents, as well as honoring each other—something that is vital if we are to be a vibrant, caring, faith community—let's get practical, and let's GET REAL.

■_■

*Cultivate real relationships based
on honesty and integrity.*

For Discussion

1. What was the function of this commandment in ancient Israel? What direct parallels can we draw from it as our average life expectancy increases?

2. When was the last time you were made to feel "less than real"? What was that experience like for you?

3. How difficult is it for us Christians, who represent God's covenant community, to value other people with love, honor, and respect, especially if they are different from us?

4. Can you identify one person or one group whom you will try to treat differently as a result of this commandment?

■

You shall not murder.

6

Rack Your Brain!
Protecting and Promoting Life

An ironic thing happened as I was racking my brain, thinking about the meaning of this commandment. A mosquito bit me on the ankle, so I killed it. The irony startled me, but it should have been no surprise. I don't have a good track record with pesky insects.

For one recent job interview, the employer's representative took me to a local steak house for dinner. The cut of meat was identifiable, but the species of origin was not. The two of us sat there, conversing while we waited for our food. Meanwhile, a fly persistently circled the area, making stops on the table or on my arm. We were involved in our own private game of "shoofly." The fly would land, and I would casually shoo it away. It would land again, and I would shoo it away. This routine continued for about five minutes.

How awkward! I was trying to be attentive and impressive to my prospective employer, but this small creature was distracting and irritating me. I gave it every opportunity to move on to the next table or even across the table, where it could vex my dinner partner. Nothing doing!

Even so, I was enjoying the interview! After all the hard work in school, here I was sitting across the table from another religious professional, getting acquainted, and talking shop. Finally I decided I had been generous enough to that pesky, winged critter. The next time it landed on my arm, I would catch it, crush it in one motion, and dump it in the ashtray. I did not want to put it in the ashtray, where its eyes could stare at us, but that seemed to be better than littering the floor with a dead insect in front of a prospective employer. Littering was an offense, at least along highways, but so far as I knew, killing an insect was not. So that was my decision: kill the fly, drop it in the ashtray, and never break eye contact with my dinner partner. I did just that. It was a swift, graceful move. No beverages spilled. No saltshakers scooted off the table. The move was perfectly executed.

I can still remember the look on my dinner partner's face as I released that dead fly into the ashtray. His bald head turned a little pink, a hint of fire appeared in his calm gray eyes, and he stretched a little more upright as he said, "You killed that fly! What kind of pacifist are you?"

To this day I do not know if he was being facetious. I figured by that point I had lost points on moral fortitude, and the best I could do was salvage the moment with creativity. I replied, "I'm a pacifist with an attitude and a limit. Next question!" But I must admit that I racked my brain for a few days after that, wondering if killing a fly was wrong.

What do you think? Are houseflies protected by the sixth commandment? Our task of understanding this brief command would be simplified if only it included a direct object. What or whom shall we not kill? Any and everything? Does that include the blood-sucking mosquito we destroy before it dines on us? Or the annoying housefly that tries to join us at the dinner table? Or the creepy crawly things that make our lives uncomfortable?

Just as we think we have solved that dilemma and are sure the commandment does not apply to insects and rodents, we encounter an activist who insists that animals have rights and the sixth command forbids us to kill and eat. At a recent conference, such a vegetarian chose to share a dinner table with me and a few friends. This person chattered all through dinner that the rest of us were cannibals because we were eating pork. Since cannibals eat their own kind, and we were eating meat from a pig, perhaps we should have been offended. I suppose, however, that comment was less insulting than being called a cannibal while eating a fruit or vegetable.

If we overcome the guilt such a person tries to cast upon us, and we are convinced the law applies only to human life, does it apply to all humans and all situations? Does this law regulate our actions if we are attacked in war, or by burglars invading our homes, or while walking around our favorite park, and find ourselves in a supposedly kill-or-be-killed situation? Opponents of abortion, capital punishment, and euthanasia frequently appeal to this commandment as lending divine support to their position. Is that an acceptable use of this law?

If only those biblical writers had included a direct object in this commandment, telling exactly who and what we cannot kill, we would be spared the effort of racking our brain. But we have been denied that luxury. It remains for us to wrestle with the letter of this law in hopes of uncovering the spirit that undergirds it.

The Old Testament Scriptures themselves do not simplify the issue for us. While the sixth commandment prohibits killing, the Old Testament itself contains enough violence to fare well in the Nielsen ratings as a made-for-TV movie. The first social crime recorded in Genesis was Cain's murder of his brother Abel. Moses, the giver of these laws, killed an Egyptian out of anger because he was abusing an Israelite brother. The book of Joshua describes how Israel entered the Promised Land in a conquest; wars were waged, and countless lives slaughtered, supposedly under God's direction and with divine blessing.

For certain crimes, the prescribed punishment was the death penalty. For instance, Exodus 21:15 and 17 say that whoever strikes or curses a parent will be put to death. Such examples show that under certain conditions, killing someone was an acceptable act in the Israelite society.

There is a recognizable drop in approval of such actions in the New Testament. Some would ascribe that to the fact that it is a higher level of revelation. Others might say the difference is that the Old Testament regulated an entire nation, which tried to be a theocratic society. The New Testament regulated an exclusively religious group within a Roman society and therefore was not faced with the same problems as were the Jews. Even so, in Acts 5, the death of Ananias and Sapphira is God's punishment because of their deception.

Even as we wrestle with the meaning of the sixth command, we must recognize that Exodus, the book containing this law, also recounts events where killing occurs, sometimes with divine authorization. So let us be forewarned against easy attempts at a universal application. If we are to benefit from the wisdom of this command, we will first have to rack our brain!

If we appeal to the Hebrew language to help us unpack the meaning of this brief law, we receive some direction—but not without remaining loose ends. The most common word for kill in the Hebrew language is *harag*. Instead of *harag*, this commandment uses *ratsakh*. That is an interesting choice because *ratsakh* has a wider range of possible meanings than does *harag*. It normally refers to murder—the willful, premeditated killing of an individual out of hatred, anger, desire, greed, or other hostile, revenge-seeking motives. Yet *ratsakh* never refers to killing in war. But *ratsakh* can also refer to unintentional homicide, as in the laws of asylum in Deuteronomy 4:41-43. That means that intentionality can no longer be the dividing line by which one keeps or breaks this command.

Negatively the command simply says, "You shall not kill," thereby depriving an individual of life, intentionally or unintentionally. Patrick Miller says, "The malicious violence that takes the life of a human being is absolutely contrary to the will of God and is destructive not only of life but of community."[1] That encourages us to consider the command from a positive perspective.

Positively, the command calls members of the faith community to recognize that life is a gift from God and is lived within God's ordering of the world and God's definition of the faith community. The Genesis creation story says that God created humans, breathed into them the breath of life, and called what he had made "very good." [2] Psalm 8 expounds on the high and lofty status that God accords to humanity. When we consider these themes, we can hardly escape the conclusion that, from a Christian perspective, there is such a thing as the "sanctity of life," human beings created in God's image.

Thus even after Cain murdered his brother, God marked him to protect him from being murdered by others out of revenge. The lesson we can learn from this is that we participate in that sanctity by living lives and ordering community in ways that protect and preserve human life, by helping sustain life rather than demeaning or harming it. If and when we decide to kill or approve of others who kill, let us acknowledge in advance that we are, in fact, acting in God's stead. That will certainly eliminate haste in the matter; it may well abolish many types of deaths that we might sanction.

Earlier I noted that in addition to literally taking the life of another, the choice of *ratsakh* includes broader forms of taking life. That is where the loose ends enter the picture. The use of *ratsakh* allows us to ask about other ways people harm other people, sometimes to the point of taking their life. Jesus raised that very issue in Matthew 5:21-26: "You have heard that it was said to the people long ago, 'Do not murder, and anyone who murders will be subject to judgment.' But I tell you that anyone who is angry with a brother or sister will be subject to judgment" (NIV/NRSV).

Jesus interpreted the sixth command to include not only acts that immediately cause death, but also actions and attitudes that harm, demean, dishearten, and take the wind out of their sails—a figurative if not literal killing.[3] At that point the spirit of the command is no longer *only* about protecting life; it is also about enhancing, contributing to, and encouraging life.

If the Christian faith is to transmit that value, we have an overwhelming task ahead of us. In this age of information and technology, the media informs us and sometimes manipulates us. Various studies claim that the average child, on reaching adolescence, will have witnessed the violent destruction of a staggering number of human lives. On any given prime-time night, scanning through the channels brings us into contact with an assortment of violence, including assaults, killings, robberies, kidnapings, murder conspiracies, arsons, extortions, bombings, and suicides.

Some of these directly take the physical life of another. The others demean, detract, and deny persons the opportunity to live in the security and confidence that they are worth something to themselves and the world at large. This is not intended to be a homily on the sins of TV. I enjoy watching it immensely when I can find something that interests me. Yet in the process of viewing these programs, our eyes, ears, and minds are being bombarded with images, stories—and *values*. This random violence and sense-less waste of life imply that life is cheap and can be wasted at will.

Much of what is being seen, heard, witnessed, and experienced is a direct contradiction of the sixth commandment. How different from Paul's counsel in Philippians 4:8, to think about things true, honorable, just, pure, pleasing, commendable, excellent, and worthy of praise! Our task becomes, first, to learn to appreciate and respect the gift of life. That means we learn to value ourselves as creations of God. But not only ourselves, for that would leave us with an egocentric world. We must also learn to value each other as brothers and sisters, as people of worth in this world. When someone or something is of worth, of value, of importance to us—then we are more careful of those persons or things.

These things have a prominent place in the covenant community of faith: honor, respect, and protection of life, and all that contributes to a healthy "sanctity of life." In considering this commandment, it now becomes insufficient to merely ask, "Have I ever killed anybody? Nah. Check that command off!" Instead, the spirit of the law encourages us to consider whether or not we are helping protect the lives of each other. It challenges us to reflect on whether or not we are enhancing the lives of others in the community, rather than tearing at each other through hostile emotions and attitudes. So this negatively stated command can in fact have a positive and healthy influence in Christian actions.

I want to suggest that we can begin to implement those positive practices by racking our brains. As used here, *rack* is also an acronym. No doubt you have heard of the term "random acts of violence." Those are basically the types of things that transgress the sixth commandment. As a counterpractice to them, I propose that we practice "*R*andom

Acts of Compassion and Kindness"—RACK. Hence the title: Rack Your Brain.

Take, for instance, this real-life example.[4] One afternoon, a woman in a red car pulled up to a toll bridge in California. She told the attendant, "I'm paying for myself and six cars behind me." One after another, the next six drivers arrived at the booth with money in hand, only to be told by the collector, "Some lady up ahead already paid your fare. Have a nice day."

As it turned out, the woman had read a note taped to a friend's refrigerator: "Practice Random Acts of Kindness and Senseless Acts of Beauty." The words leapt out at her, so she wrote them down and began to live them out. *Practice random acts of kindness and senseless acts of beauty! Rack your brain!* With the grace of God and leading of the Holy Spirit, I suspect we can arrive at more significant random acts of compassion and kindness than merely paying highway tolls. The assumption is that kindness can build on itself as much as violence can.

We keep the sixth commandment best when our understanding of the sanctity of life not only produces abstinence from violence but also promotes compassion and kindness. As members of a covenant faith community, that is how the commandment challenges us today. Let us embody both the positive and negative sides of this commandment as we protect life as well as bless each other with kindness.

■
□

Enhance the lives of others with random acts of compassion and kindness.

For Discussion

1. How do we resolve the apparent contradiction of a commandment saying "you shall not murder" contained in a book that occasionally authorizes killing?

2. What justification is given in this chapter for expanding the meaning of the word *kill* beyond a literal loss of life?

3. How does the concept of "sanctity of life" make this a relevant commandment even for those who have never killed another person?

4. What are some appropriate *R*andom *A*cts of Compassion and *K*indness that you can do today that will help you keep this commandment? RACK your brain.

■▪

You shall not commit adultery.

7

Slippery Steps
The Danger of Compromising Situations

You will be relieved to know that although I prefer to use personal experience as a vehicle for communicating the truth contained in Scripture, I do not have a wealth of material upon which to draw for the subject of adultery. In this case, a few comparisons will have to suffice.

One useful way of approaching this commandment is with the imagery of a slippery step. I do have some experience with those. During those hot, humid North Carolina summers, the kids in the Marshall household always hoped to visit a place called White Lake. Natural springs fed the lake. It got its name from the fact that the water was so clear, a person could see straight through to the bottom, covered with white sands.

When we vacationed there, our days were spent doing cannonballs and bellyflops, lurking under the pier in hopes of scaring anyone who strolled past, and slowly edging into deeper water only to be summoned back to the shore by our parents. Now I should say that *deep* in this case was only about five feet down, but when you are a four-foot nub and your swimming skills are topped out at the doggy-paddle level, five feet is plenty deep.

Even so, there was one place where I could play in the deeper water. At the end of the pier was a large gazebo, with old weathered steps and a handrail descending into the water. I loved to play there. Waves from nearby boats would lap against my little body, jerking it back and forth. But the best thing about playing on those steps was a gift from Mother Nature. They were covered with green moss, nature's way of carpeting those old wooden steps and adding a bit of beauty to a potential eyesore.

From the moss came an extra benefit—or problem, depending on one's point of view: it made the steps slippery. Once seated on the steps, my wiggling and sliding sent me tumbling into the five feet of water. Down I would plunge until I hit the lake bottom. The water closed over my head, leaped down my throat, and shot up my nose, baptizing me in the name of who knows what. All I needed was a minister to make it official, except for the fact that I did not feel renewed as I pulled myself back up the steps.

All I could manage to do was cough and spit and try to soothe the burning sensation on my back created by a mixture of scrapes and sand. Instead of getting out of the water like someone with an ounce of common sense, I would climb the steps again and return to my seat. Not five minutes later, I would again be eating sand at the bottom of the lake.

One thing seems certain when it comes to dealing with slippery steps. Despite whatever "fun" they initially offer, they have a habit of always leaving us somewhere we do not want to be. Like on the bottom of the lake drinking dirty water and eating swirling sand. Or sitting in a mud puddle with gooey water seeping into every crack it can find. Or lying on your back on the ice, staring at the sky and praying no one saw you fall. Slippery steps always find a way to threaten, if not rob us, of a sense of balance. Slippery steps are not limited to the realm of gravity and physical movement. Many of the choices we make may lead us along paths lined with one slippery step after another. They deprive us of our balance and generally leave us somewhere we do not want to be, or perhaps where we want to be but should not be. We simply have no business getting involved in some things, no matter how intriguing, enticing, or tempting they may be. Even the apostle Paul recognized that when he said that in the life of grace, everything was lawful for Christians, but not everything was helpful (1 Cor. 6:12). He had in mind that we would try to discern the difference.

Continually choosing to play on slippery steps results in a condition similar to the guy who had a bad burn on each side his head. His friend asked how that happened. He explained that he had ironed his clothes that morning and was rushing around getting ready for work. In the midst of that mad dash, the phone rang and he accidentally answered the hot iron instead of the phone.

The friend said, "Well, that explains one side. How did you burn the other one?" The fellow said, "They called back a second time." That is similar to what happens when we insist on playing on the slippery steps. We get burned time after time after time as we repeatedly lose our balance and fall.

The seventh commandment addresses a slippery step that was a problem in ancient Israelite society and is just as slippery today. When its advice is ignored, quite often the result is loss of balance that causes individuals, families, and even communities to fall.

This commandment prohibits adultery. Such a prohibition presupposes an understanding of marriage, because without the latter, the former is pointless. The Israelite institution of marriage was a bit different from ours. Polygamy was allowed, although we do not know how widespread the practice actually was. Sometimes a marriage was dissolved, and the law contained guidelines describing when that was appropriate in Israel. But so long as the marriage was intact, certain standards were to be respected.

Abstaining from adultery was one of those guidelines, although a double standard existed in that patriarchal society. The law forbade wives from having sexual relations with anyone other than their husband. In contrast, men were not to have relations with the wives of other men. Any modern consideration of this command needs to eliminate double standards and operate in an egalitarian manner.

Though our starting place may be slightly different than that of ancient Israel, life in our faith community continues to recognize this commandment as legitimate for us as well. The words of the wedding ceremony state, "Marriage is an honorable estate instituted by God. . . ." Ideally, marriage is a pledge of faith, a commitment to care, a promise of a lasting union. The church still considers marriage as a sacred covenant made between a man and a woman, in the presence of God and the witnessing community.

Ideally, this special commitment is a covenant of love and honor, of passion and compassion, of intimate community between two people. But in reality, even with divine blessing and high expectations, marriages are not necessarily "made in heaven." Even if they are, so are thunder and lightning! As someone once said, "Marriages are not made in heaven. They come in kits, and you have to put them together."

This seventh commandment needs to be a part of the kit. Marriage stakes out the claim of the two partners in marriage to a relationship between themselves that is not to be compromised or destroyed by the action of either partner. This command is designed to keep us off one of the slippery steps that would rob us of our balance and compromise the marriage covenant. At a basic level, this law prohibits sexual relations with anyone other than the marriage partner. It is designed to guard the sanctity of the marriage relationship, and it recognizes that the sexual relationship is a prominent factor in an intimate marriage.

The damage inflicted by this slippery step, however, is not just about sex with someone other than the marriage partner. The covenant of marriage includes a pledge of fidelity to one another; consequently, adultery dishonors that pledge. As it does so, adultery also becomes an issue of trust and betrayal. Where trust is betrayed, intimacy evaporates. Where intimacy evaporates, community can be nothing more than fantasy. Where community is fantasy, marriage is a tragedy. Such situations, gradually or suddenly, destroy marital relations and start a destructive chain reaction.

It is possible that in the focus on self-needs, one may believe adultery involves or hurts no one but the two parties involved. But in fact it is clear that many innocent people are crushed in the process, with the damage ranging from emotional fallout to the spreading of AIDS. Adultery is about more than what is lost between two people. It also involves larger family systems, which are further linked to community relationships. It not only complicates the home; it also destabilizes the community.

In the Israelite clan-based, tribal affiliated community, stable home lives were essential if the community itself was to remain stable. By that, I do not only mean stability within the family; I also mean stability between families. That would be difficult to maintain if husbands were involved with wives other than the one to whom they are married.

In addition to whatever intimacy and trust violations occur between the married couple, adultery skews the relational neighborhood. Sociologists recognize that in addition to our geographical neighborhood, which is the area in which we physically live, we are also involved in a relational neighborhood. It is composed of people with whom we have significant ties and relations even if we are not in the same geographic neighborhood. We may live on Main Street in Our Town. Yet our vocation, our friends, and the majority of our social activities may occur in Another Place. That other place would be a significant relational neighborhood. Some trust, intimacy, and security exist in that relational neighborhood—at least until adultery enters the picture.

Adultery twists the emotional neighborhood into knots. It triangulates channels of intimacy. The end result is that suspicion, anger, and even indifference creep into the relational neighborhood. Those things make it difficult for a community to survive. What was said with regard to a couple applies to a community as well: Where trust is betrayed, intimacy evaporates. Where intimacy evaporates, community can be nothing more than fantasy. Where community is a fantasy but people insist on being a group anyway, life will be filled with misery. That slippery step seemed so enticing, that act of adultery so appealing. But it strips us of our balance and dumps us in a place where we cannot possibly want to live if we have any desire to know and live the Truth.

Recognizing slippery steps for what they truly are is sometimes difficult because we live in a society that trivializes sexuality by equating it almost exclusively with seduction. Few parents socialize their children about sexuality the way they do about religion or politics. The church has often been guilty of promoting such a negative view of sexuality that its members sometimes feel it must be merely tolerated as a weakness of the flesh rather than celebrated as a God-created and approved part of our humanity. When the family and the church fail in this area, their members are left uneducated and vulnerably receptive to the teachings of the TV and entertainment industries. They bombard us with an array of ideas about gender and sexuality, most of which are detrimental to couples and communities. Subliminal promises of youth and virility underlie our advertising in every medium. Seduction and sensuality are used to sell everything from cola to cars and Cool Whip. Consequently, the seventh commandment seems prudish and obsolete. I don't agree and I hope you don't either.

Negatively, the seventh commandment says members of the faith community who seek to live and order their lives according to God's desires shall not commit adultery. Positively, it acknowledges that sexual involvement provides a way for two persons to share the mutuality of their love. When that love is exclusive, it builds up each partner. The second command recognizes that no community can stay together when there is an easy disregard for the covenant relationship in marriage. Without fidelity between husband and wife, many disruptive consequences arise.

Do you see why the seventh command deserves a place among the covenant regulations and needs to be respected by members of the faith community? It is not about denying sexuality. It is not intended to deprive anyone of their sexuality. The goal is to have a healthy expression of sexuality that respects the covenant of marriage and strengthens the faith community, as individuals navigate around the slippery step of infidelity.

Respect the covenant of mutual love.

For Discussion

1. What are the ways in which adultery is more than merely sexual infidelity?

2. Why is adultery detrimental to a community's stability?

3. Has the church done its part to make adultery less likely among its members? What can be done differently?

4. Are there ways you can be more respectful of the covenant of mutual love?

■■

You shall not steal.

8

(   )

Disregarding Boundaries

When we lived in North Carolina, Judi and I looked forward to summer. It was a season of excused absences from seminary classes, celebrated with meal after countless meal of garden-fresh vegetables. But most of all, we loved summers because we spent them in the parsonage of the Edward Hill Meeting, where I was pastoring, rather than in our Durham apartment. Majestic oaks, lush pastures, and an assortment of wildlife surrounded our summer home. Best of all, it was located on a quiet road outside a crossroad community named Bonlee. We found it a pleasant task to leave behind the city of Durham for a summer of simplicity and solitude.

As Judi and I enjoyed one hot July, we decided a few days at the beach were in order. About four o'clock the day before we were to leave, we drove into a town called Siler City to purchase necessary supplies like suntan lotion, soft drinks, and the essential beach Frisbee. While we were there, we had dinner, because dining out in Bonlee meant ordering an overcooked hot dog at the only convenience store located at the crossroads. Our whole trip took less than three hours.

We brought home our bodies fueled with excitement, our car fueled with gas, and our minds eager for packing bags so we could leave early the next morning. In the best of spirits, we traveled down that quiet, peaceful road, headed for home. As we turned into the driveway, we beheld an unexpected sight—our front door was standing wide open. Our eyes grew large, and we laughed in amazement. Look what we did! We went off and left our door standing open. That was a silly thing to do. Next time, why not just hang out a sign that reads, "Take our stuff, please!"

I said to Judi, "I don't remember leaving that door open. Did you do that?"

She said, "I didn't do it. You must have."

Uh-oh.

With more than a little trepidation, I peeked into the house. Inside, I saw a combination of contradictions. Some things were in places where they did not belong: clothes strewn all over the floor and lamps overturned. Some things were not where they belonged, such as the TV and the microwave. In their place were empty spaces, like the one at the beginning of this chapter where you expected to find the chapter title. That is what it would look like if someone stole the title—only an empty space would remain.

During the three hours we were away from the house, someone came into our home and stole several things from us. If any of you have ever had something stolen, you know the sickening feelings that accompany this crime. The thieves' actions left behind more than empty places that once held such possessions as our TV, our microwave, my Guilford college class ring, and an engraved pocket watch that Judi gave me for our first anniversary. They also left behind empty feelings that spawned queasy emotions like fear, anxiety, and uneasiness the way a mud hole breeds mosquitoes.

I remember how difficult it was to sleep that night, wondering if the thieves would return. In all honesty, I wanted to sleep with a gun next to the bed, except that we did not own any. However, I put the baseball bat within arm's reach. I figured my faith might not let me shoot them, but if they got close enough and I had a sudden lapse of faith, I would be ready for a little batting practice.

Someone somewhere is wearing a fourteen-carat gold, black onyx, 1985 Guilford college class ring, with the initials JWM engraved inside. And they didn't crack a single book, write the first paper, or take any exams to earn the right to wear it. Someone is keeping track of time with a pocket watch whose engraved date has absolutely no significance to them. They do not have a clue how precious that watch really is, because its value to me is calculated in a manner other than dollars and cents.

Someone sits at the end of the day, props up his or her feet, and watches a Sony TV. Frankly, I was glad to get rid of it, because its best days were long passed. I only wish the thieves had taken the outdated stereo whose best features are a turntable and an eight-track tape player. If there is anything worse than a thief, it is a selective thief! But the real point is that someone somewhere has our stuff!

To steal. To take something from another person. To take something that is clearly not your own and keep it, without permission. The eighth commandment simply says, "Don't do that."

The mere possibility of stealing requires, first of all, a concept of ownership, private property, in contrast to communal ownership. If ownership grants access to certain people while denying access to others, that means ownership establishes boundaries accompanied by restricted entry.

When I lived in Durham, one of the most difficult adjustments for me in renting an apartment was an adjustment to the boundaries in apartment living. If someone passed by the window, I noticed and looked to see who that person was. Hundreds of people lived there, so I seldom knew who they were. It took a while to realize that, in the rural area where I grew up, property boundaries were such that if someone passed by close to your window, you had better know who they were! But the boundaries in apartment living are different. Strangers passed by my window, played in front of my apartment, and occasionally even sat on my front steps. In apartment living, those things are to be expected.

The boundaries of ownership, however, specify that some are and some are not entitled to possess, utilize, and control the things that are owned. Some people choose not to respect those boundaries. For example, one hotel reported that during the first ten months in its operation, the following items were stolen: thirty-eight thousand spoons. What kind of place settings require only spoons? Hotel guests stole eighteen hundred silver coffee pots. Perhaps the spoons were needed to stir the coffee poured from these pots. Fifteen hundred silver finger bowls disappeared during those first ten months. And believe it or not, one hundred Bibles were stolen as well.

It is sad when a person steals something that *says* "Thou shalt not steal." I guess if God ever prints another version, the don't-steal part should be closer to the front. A thief probably doesn't have time to read all the way to Exodus twenty before deciding whether or not to take the book.

About four million people are caught shoplifting each year in the United States alone. The figures for all of North America are even more astounding. But for every person caught, it is estimated that thirty-five go undetected. That, however, considers only the most commonly agreed upon type of stealing.

Those figures do not measure times when persons refuse to work and exploit agencies meant to help the truly needy. In such cases, the culprit robs the needy as well as the taxpayers who fund those programs. Neither do they measure those who interpret God's gift of dominion to mean that humanity has divine permission to exploit and ruin our environment for profit. In the process, these thieves steal health and life, threatening our very survival. Yet consider the shameful mountains of waste we dispose of, while ignoring the cries of the poor and famine-stricken. Isn't this a form of stealing as well?

The implications of the command, "You shalt not steal," are almost mind-boggling. However, we do not have to think in such monumental proportions to learn from the eighth commandment.

There are, in fact, several dimensions to this command. When we think of theft, loss of property is probably the first thing that comes to mind. However, many Bible scholars believe this command was first directed to kidnapping instead of personal property. The reality of that possibility is driven home by Exodus 21:16, which reads "Anyone who kidnaps another and either sells him or still has him when he is caught must be put to death."

Ironically, as civilized as we supposedly are, we frequently read of kidnappings. Posters, milk cartons, and news bulletins remind us that some people have their lives stolen from them. Some are returned in exchange for a ransom; others may be sold into black-market slavery. Sometimes we never hear from them again. This form of theft actually robs life from the one who is kidnapped. It takes their freedom, their chance of pursuing their goals. It robs their family and loved ones of someone significant. It is a hideous form of theft. The empty space it leaves behind is the complete absence of the life once there.

Another form of theft is more common—to steal a person's possessions. In Israel, it was probably a goat, a calf, or a basket of grain. Or perhaps a cloak, flask, or a lamp. Today it would more likely be a wallet, silver, or an antique—though I actually did hear of a couple of bandits who stole a full-grown cow in a Chevette hatchback, if you can believe that![1] My feeling is that if they could squeeze that bovine into the car *and* close the lid, they probably had earned their prize.

Israel understood property to be an extension of the self of the owner. So do we, to some extent. Consequently, the theft of property is a violation of the person, not just their wealth. It is more than the loss of something that was *mine!* The loss may well deprive a person of the ability to make ends meet, to survive and prosper. This was true in Israel from the standpoint that the things stolen often were almost always directly related to the provision of basic subsistence needs. Such theft immediately leaves empty spaces in the place the possession once occupied. Those holes usually become more noticeable in the following days. They are not easily filled.

Third, and connected to the previous two, is the theft of privilege. It is not just a matter of stealing people or property. The loss of those things reduces the possibility of a satisfied or abundant life. Without the goat, the grain, or contents of the wallet, it is difficult to provide the basic essentials of life. Through taking the antiques, the class ring, the pocket watch, theft leaves empty spaces in our lives and weakens our memories. When someone steals from us, our security is violated and our trust is betrayed. Life becomes a bit uneasy and fearful for a while.

I think it is safe to say that the loss of possessions only scratches the surface of the reasons behind this prohibition. More important than the objects that are lost is the boundary that is violated. More precious than the value of the stolen property is the peace that is kidnapped. In fact, it has been said that theft is a type of enslavement caused by the complete domination of one human being by another.[2] To this point, the covenant described in these ten commandments has been about creating a community, establishing an identity, and developing guidelines for relationships among the community's participants. It has defined the faith community's center as the God who called us and who gives us the ability to live as a covenant community. It has conveyed key qualities such as honor and integrity that guide our interactions with each other. This command moves a step further. It is not out of line to say that the spirit of this command is about respect.

Where groups congregate, boundaries will develop. These include geographical boundaries that designate property. Things within those boundaries belong to a particular person. They are off-limits to the world unless that person decides to share them. But let us recognize that boundaries in a community also include behavioral ones as well. Boundaries serve to delineate acceptable types of interaction between persons. These may include such things as types of touching, conversation, or even arguing.

When we trespass into those protected areas, the chances are great that we will steal something in the process. Perhaps it is a possession. Maybe it is trust. It could be something invisible yet essential to individual and community health, such as dignity or peace of mind. Stealing disrupts the community because community is expected to be a safe place in which its people are nurtured and supported and built up. But stealing is tearing down, destroying the trust level, and shaking our support systems.

Negatively, the eighth command says, "You shall not steal." It can be stated positively by saying that, in the faith community, we are called to recognize and respect other people's boundaries. We can even go a step further and realize that as our lives intersect together, we should help create a climate of generosity that prefers to give to others rather than take from them. In the faith community, not only is stealing wrong, but so is withholding if we have the opportunity to minister and make a difference. Let me tell you a story to illustrate.

Long ago, a village priest prepared for a major religious celebration. But he discovered that the wine barrel was completely empty. That was the kind of empty space that could ruin the occasion. To remedy this situation as quickly as possible, he asked every family in the village community to bring a flask of good wine and pour it into the barrel. This seemed like an agreeable solution to the townspeople. One by one they hurried home to choose their best wine. But as one fellow looked over the many fine wines he possessed, he began to feel sorry that he would have to give any of it away. Thinking that if just one person withheld wine, it would not be noticeable, he decided to pour water into the barrel. With each family's contribution the barrel was quickly filled and the festivities could begin.

The next morning when the high point in the worship service arrived, the priest pried the lid from the barrel and used his dipper to fill each person's goblet. However, instead of seeing rich dark red wine, the liquid he poured from the barrel was clear plain water. Apparently most of the people had refused to give from their wine, thinking it would not make any difference to pour in a little water instead. Now the community was robbed of a special time of festivity and fellowship. Withholding can be an inverted form of stealing; the end result deprives everyone involved.

From missing titles to burglarized homes and empty wine barrels, let us learn about the unsettling and sometimes disastrous effects of empty spaces created by thievery. Let us recognize that in the faith community, God asks us to respect one another through what we do not steal, as well as through what we share.

■₁

Respect other persons' boundaries.

For Discussion

1. What types of theft can occur in our society? Are there ways the church can address this problem?

2. What are some "legalized" forms of theft, such as unnecessary waste of resources, in which you currently participate? What are some immediate steps you can take to begin sharing rather than stealing in these areas?

3. What personal boundaries do you want for other members of the faith community to respect?

■□

You shall not give false testimony
against your neighbor.

9
———————

The Real Story
The Importance of Truth Telling

The ninth commandment states, "You shall not give false testimony against your neighbor." Or, as the more-popular, shortened, version bluntly says, "You shall not lie." It sounds plain and simple: tell the truth. But from a community-building perspective, the motive for the command is as important as the command itself.

The point is illustrated nicely in a fairly familiar tale with a slightly different slant.[1] Jon Scieszka's version of "The Three Little Pigs" tells the story from the wolf's point of view. In this retelling, the wolf claims to have been framed. He was simply seeking to borrow a cup of sugar to use in a cake he was making for his granny. A sneezing attack caused by a common cold, rather than malice, led to the destruction of the first two houses and the deaths of the first two pigs. Since he liked pork, it seemed a shame to waste a good dinner. The news media's misrepresentation of the facts to make a good story led to the "blow your house down" stuff and portrayed an innocent canine as a big bad wolf. The *real* story, according to Scieszka's version, is that the wolf was framed!

This retelling of a classic fairy tale illustrates an important point: there is usually more than one side to every story. In fact, many have aptly noted that there are always three sides to every story—his side, her side, and the truth. Sometimes the truth seems as clear as black and white. But on other occasions, a cloudy shade of gray overcasts the truth, and no matter how much we try, we cannot gain clear insight in the matter. Difficult or not, truth telling is the goal of this ninth commandment: "You shall not give false testimony against your neighbor."

Literally, the Hebrew reads, "You shall not respond or answer against your neighbor falsely." Two immediate observations should grab our attention. The first is only obvious in the Hebrew text. The verb *'anah* is usually translated as "respond." It can, however, also mean "oppress" or "afflict" or "put down." So we could read this verse, "You shall not oppress your neighbor by lying." Lying is not merely spinning a yarn to free us from a tight spot. Lying will usually oppress the other person as well. An erroneous story accepted as truth labels a person for life.

I sadly witnessed this in the life of an African-American excon who wanted a fresh start but was continually under suspicion for every incident of theft that occurred in our community. With a sense of grief, I heard about it as a young man with a colorful past told me that he once felt called into the ministry and reformed his lifestyle through God's grace. Eventually he abandoned all hope because his home church chose to perpetuate his past rather than celebrate his future. With remorse, I see it happen on a regular basis when adolescents perpetuate stories of permissiveness about their peers to serve their own selfish purposes. The wolf's version of what *really* happened to those little pigs mirrors real life.

Stories can be twisted and misconstrued, giving another person a bad reputation. Because reputations influence how we receive and treat other people, lying produces consequences in the life of the one to whom or about whom the lie was told. Those consequences can be nothing short of oppressive; they create a continual burden that must be endured.

The second thing that grabs our attention is the command's inclusion of the neighbor. On the one hand, lying is problematic because it amounts to deceit on the part of the liar. Deceit is not a virtuous characteristic, except perhaps for the magician. When I think about the problems associated with lies, I think first in terms of integrity and honesty. But the commandment does not focus on those issues. Instead, it emphasizes that lying is a social evil, not a private one. It teaches that the worst victim is the neighbor, which is to say, the one to whom or about whom the lie was told.

There is probably no lie we can tell that does not, in some way, affect others. At least, when we spread false information, it limits the hearer's ability to make an informed decision because he or she does not have an accurate report. Truthfulness helps insure freedom of choice; not until we know the correct information are we in a position to evaluate all the available options.

At its worst, a lie manipulates our choices, our emotions, and our responses. Have you ever been lied about? Have you felt that people were saying or believing things about you that were not the real story? Can you remember how they made you feel, and some of the responses they provoked within you? As lies channel our responses along certain paths, they eventually affect our reputation. Sometimes they affect us directly by the untruths they spread, and sometimes indirectly by the poorly informed choices we make because of the false information.

A series of choices makes a lifestyle. What others observe about our lifestyle becomes our reputation. It is an oppressive task to battle a false reputation, like being labeled a big, bad wolf, or a thief, when in fact the real story reveals something different.

In the covenant community, lying is prohibited because of what it does to the recipients of the lie. The eighth commandment protects the neighbor as well as the neighbor's reputation. It insures the neighbor's freedom to make an informed choice and therefore helps the neighbor to decide and act with integrity.

How often are we denied those things? There are many places in our society where the atmosphere exudes a casual acceptance of lying. Advertisers make claims about products that are not completely true, so we buy them under false pretenses. The media sometimes reports events with biases that shape how we understand the truth; consequently, we formulate a position or opinion based on a shaky foundation. Sometimes, an individual spreads outright lies about another individual simply because one disagrees or dislikes the other. If we are the spread-er, we are vicious and spiteful; if we are the spread-ee, we are afflicted and burdened for the wrong reasons. One place where we must guarantee we are telling the truth is in the courtroom. But even there, lawyers are expected to find loopholes that allow the facts to be seen in another light, thereby reshaping the *real* story! Accessing the truth is not always easy.

Although I do not want to romanticize Israelite morals, ancient Israel had no place for such a casual approach to truth and lying, especially in their law courts. If they discovered a person was giving worthless testimony about another, the law required that the liar receive the penalty that the one about whom the lie was told would have been subject to, if the testimony had been true. In some cases that meant death; in others it meant threefold or fourfold restitution. If those sound like extreme penalties (and they do), that only illustrates the seriousness of false testimony in the context of their faith community. They understood that far-reaching consequences accompany lies.

Once the lies are spread and the damage is done, it is impossible to reverse their effects completely. A story is told of a farmer's wife who spread a slanderous story about her pastor throughout the village. Soon the whole countryside had heard it, drawn certain conclusions based on it, and began to act in accord with those conclusions.

Later the woman became sick. Thinking she was about to die and wanting to get her affairs in order, she confessed that the story was untrue. After that startling confession, *she recovered!* After her recovery, she came to the pastor and begged his pardon. The old pastor said, "Of course, I will gladly pardon you if you will comply with a wish of mine." The woman agreed to his condition.

The pastor instructed her, "Go home, kill a black hen, pluck the feathers, put them in a basket, and bring them here." In a half hour she returned, having completed the task.

The pastor said, "Now, go through the village, and at each street corner, scatter a few of these feathers. Take the remaining ones to the top of the church bell tower and scatter them to the winds. Then return to me."

After the woman did that, she returned to the pastor. He said, "Now, go through the village and gather the feathers again and see that not a single one is missing."

The woman just looked at him with astonishment and groaned, "Why, that is impossible! The wind has scattered them over the fields everywhere. I cannot possibly recover them all."

The pastor replied, "Yes, that is true. So while I gladly forgive you, do not forget that it is just as impossible to undo the damage your untrue words have done as it is to collect those scattered feathers."

The oppressive effects of lying are well documented. The prime example of this is one of the first stories in the Bible (Gen. 3). The serpent lied to Eve, telling her that the only reason God forbade them to eat of the tree of knowledge was because God was jealous and did not want the humans to know what the deity knows and thus become godlike. This was a lie that created oppressive results.

There are other examples in both the Old and New Testament stories that show consequences as severe as death, such as what happened to Ananias and Sapphira (Acts 5) as a result of lying to the apostles. When we consider the lessons of these stories, we will begin to see just how right Jesus was when he said, "Simply let your 'Yes' be 'Yes,' and your 'No' [be] 'No'; anything beyond this comes from the evil one" (Matt. 5:37; cf. James 5:12).

We could argue for hours about the benefits of telling white lies occasionally, or of times when we should keep quiet because the truth is too harmful or damaging. This command does not map out how we should behave in such instances. If the only reason we wish to speak truthfully to or about someone is to hurt them, we should reexamine our motives before we open our mouths.

Although the ninth commandment doesn't map out our appropriate response to every situation, this command does insist that in the faith community, telling the *real* story should be our redeemed nature. Truth telling should be the rule rather than the exception. When the truth is not sought or proclaimed, no society can operate on the basis of mutual trust. Community formation, which is the goal of this covenant, would quickly reach an impasse because trust is essential to community formation. Perhaps thoughts such as those were behind Paul's words: "So then, putting away falsehood, let all of us speak the truth to our neighbors, for we are members of one another" (Eph. 4:25, NRSV).

As we share our lives in the faith community, we are building a network of relationships. Truth telling is a key to their endurance. We carry within us the capacity to help or to hurt the people on the opposite end of those relationships with the words we say about one another. So let us be careful to know the *real* story before we speak. Otherwise, we may misrepresent the truth and oppress those who are the subject of our conversations. In the process, we label innocent parties and alienate them, as could be the case with the Big Bad Wolf. Worse yet, it could happen to a real human being.

■▪

Truth telling shall be redeemed nature for you.

For Discussion

1. How is the act of telling a lie a social evil, rather than a purely private one?

2. What effect does lying have on a community founded on trust and respect?

3. Are there occasions that call for less than total honesty? If so, how do you reconcile them with this commandment?

4. Try to think of at least one way you have recently been dishonest. What were its lasting effects? What can you now do to reverse these effects?

■▪

**You shall not covet your neighbor's
house. You shall not covet your neighbor's wife,
or his manservant or maidservant,
his ox or donkey, or anything
that belongs to your neighbor.**

10

Fool's Gold

Learning to Appreciate Who You Are

Glitter and grandeur grab our attention, but they often exaggerate their worth. A classmate of mine taught me that lesson several years ago. He brought a small, shiny rock to Show and Tell one day. It glittered under the lights, leaving all his classmates awestruck. He told us it was fool's gold, though in fact the color was more like platinum than gold. We were good little capitalists. Fool or no fool, gold was gold, and we all wanted a piece.

Little chunks of similar looking material were mashed into the asphalt pavement in the school parking lot. Our classmate told us they also were fool's gold, but I do not know if that was the truth. I do know that every day on the way to and from the gym, we saw the brilliant reflection created as the sun's light struck the fool's gold anchored in the pavement.

Different students would try to pry a piece from the pavement and thus stake our claim to fame. Occasionally someone was successful. When that happened, the rest of us wanted a piece so badly we could hardly stand it. It was one thing to share the desire; it was a different story when one person's desire was fulfilled while the rest of us suffered and hoped. Some even tried to steal the fool's gold from those fortunate enough to possess it.

It is comical to think about that now. On one hand, we were certain it was worth something because the word *gold* was part of its name. We conveniently ignored that *fool* was also part of the label. Gold was valuable. That precious metal was worth owning, and we wanted it. On the other hand, what made it most desirable was that someone else had it. They had it, and they were receiving lots of attention because of it. Fool's gold seemed to contribute to their general status, their happiness, their self-worth. But that was more a matter of perception than reality.

The rest of the reality was that fool's gold was more attractive than it was valuable. Even then, it was most attractive from a distance. The closer we were to it, the less spectacular it seemed. After owning a piece for a day or two, fool's gold was passé. It was old news. We began to see its true value, or lack thereof. For the most part, it was valueless. Fool's gold was an appropriate name because only a fool would chase after it, and only a fool would believe that possessing it could improve the owner's life. Fool's gold and coveting have a lot in common.

At first we may wonder why there is a commandment on stealing and another on coveting since their territory seems to overlap. There is one primary difference. Stealing is linked completely to the act itself. Someone has something that we want to have for ourselves, so we take it without permission. Coveting, however, has more to do with an attitude deep within. It involves desires so strong that, to satisfy those desires, we are willing to reach out and take, or to commit other unacceptable acts.

After nine commands that either focus on God or out-er behavior, the tenth command enters the realm of the heart and mind. Those parts of the person are also subject to the claims of the covenant. Individual and community moral and ethical responsibilities are not confined to our outward behavior.

Coveting does not focus upon outward, visible actions. It concentrates instead upon a person's thoughts, motives, and attitudes. Our thoughts motivate and inspire us. We will usually act upon them in some way, sooner or later. As a result, covetousness breeds discontent and easily leads to abuse and crime.

The story of Henrietta Garrett illustrates the results of a covetous spirit. Henrietta was a woman who lived alone and had no more than a handful of friends. When she died at the age of eighty-one, she had no will and a $17-million-dollar estate. That caused one of the most fantastic cases of inheritance litigation in history. Henrietta had only one relative—a second cousin, and as I said, few friends. Yet, because of covetous spirits, over 2,600 people attempted to prove a relationship and lay claim to her fortune.

Listen to these astounding figures. The would-be relatives came from forty-seven states and twenty-nine foreign countries and were represented by more than three thousand lawyers. These people claimed to be Henrietta's relatives, all because they coveted what had belonged to her.[1]

Joshua 7 gives us another example of coveting. This event occurs after the Israelite victory at Jericho. An Israelite by the name of Achan took part of the captured treasures for himself, although God had commanded the Israelites not to keep anything at all for themselves. After his theft was discovered, Achan confessed and admitted, "I coveted them and took them." As a result of the covet-produced greed, Achan's entire family was executed. They no doubt knew that the booty was concealed in the tent and shared corporate responsibility and guilt.

A few centuries later, the prophet Micah (2:2) cried that Israelites were breaking this command as the rich and unjust oppressors of his day coveted the land of the poor. Theft and oppression arose out of that covetous spirit.

Jesus gave us a clear illustration of coveting when he encountered the rich fool, described in the Gospel of Luke (12:13-15). A man who came to hear him asked Jesus to instruct the man's brother to divide the family inheritance with him. Jesus replied, "Who set me to be a judge or arbitrator over you?" He then turned and spoke to the crowd: "Take care! Be on your guard against all kinds of greed; for one's life does not consist in the abundance of possessions." Coveting is a spirit, a conviction, a belief that what others possess will bring real meaning into lives, if only we can manage to acquire them.

There is an important thing we need to recognize, and it is crucial to understanding the positive message this command offers. Coveting is not primarily about money or even possessions. It can be rooted in many things such as pride, anxiety, and seeking power. These things are all united by a common thread: self-identity. At the heart of coveting is the lack of a clear, positive self-image.

If we listen closely to the cries of the world around us, we know many people have an image problem. Some of the more drastic cases wind up in courtrooms or therapy sessions or on TV talk shows. If we look and listen closely, we may even see and hear such a cry when we gaze in the mirror. The absence of a positive self-image, more than anything else, will drive a person to covet. Those covetous desires will erupt in the urge to accumulate other things, other representations, other symbols, all of which are used to tell others who and what we are.

But the truth is that these are little more than fool's gold. They never bring to us the real value or security or support that we desperately want. Strip away all those symbols, take away all the props by which a person often convinces oneself and others that they are somebody, and these things and symbols will have produced little change.

The tenth commandment and Jesus are correct in warning us against covetousness. Yet, it is easy for us to fall prey to the coveting spirit today, wanting all that we see. That is partially because people and places in our society tell us how bad or poor or useless we are. They do this more times than they contribute to a positive self-image and sense of worth. Our consumer-oriented society has created an infinity of things for people to want. Several are valuable but nonessential. As for many others—well, it is being polite to say that many others are useless.

Consider the hair-care industry. It is one thing for groups like the "Hair Club for Men" to provide hairpieces. That is nonessential but apparently valuable for some men's self-image. But then check the commercials for "spray-on hair." Talk about useless! Who thought of this? The fact anyone would develop such a product requires an assumption that people without hair are so envious and covetous of those who have hair that they would actually spray-paint their heads to create the illusion that they have hair. I would prefer that my hair stay in my head rather than in my comb, but it is not that important. I am a long way from spray-painting (especially since I am more efficient with a paintbrush or roller).

That is just one example. On every side we are bombarded by subliminal advertising messages that promise all the things we do not or cannot have, but which society says we should want more than anything: things like exorbitant wealth, perfect health, painless living, among others. Furthermore, these messages are meant not just to get us to want things but to make us believe that we cannot live without them! This only contributes to the already-present covetous spirit that creates bumper stickers like "The one who has the most toys when he dies wins the game."

From the negative, "thou shall not" perspective, coveting is not about not wanting something we *need*. It is about craving something we want, which also happens to be something somebody else has. It advises against becoming so obsessed and anxious over the things we lack that we are ready to take whatever action and risks necessary to gain them, even if it means taking it from someone else. But guess what! It's only fool's gold.

Coveting is the deep desire that places trust in things, thinking that they will give our lives meaning. It is the spirit that bases life's security on all the things we can gather. But if and when we do acquire something for a covetous reason, honest introspection will discover that the things we coveted do not bring all, if any, of the benefits we expected. Even if they bring temporary satisfaction, they will not heal the deep insecurities that created the covetous desire.

All of this is not to say that we cannot have things. Keeping the tenth commandment does not mean that we have to take a vow of poverty and take no thought for tomorrow. What the prohibition against coveting does mean is that we must distinguish between what is wholesome, good, and beneficial on one hand; and what only feeds a hunger for more than we need, on the other hand. Faithfulness to the covenant involves not only avoiding certain types of actions, but also certain intentions and attitudes toward others in relationship. Though that may sound difficult, it is possible in the life of faith lived according to covenant standards.

Remember, the covenant relationship with God and with the community shapes identity. The covenant is founded on an act of divine grace which demonstrates that God has chosen and accepted those who live according to the covenant. That truth alone should begin to reshape our identity and help us to keep the covenant in ways that strengthen the community.

Identity contributes to feelings of self-worth. Self-worth helps create contentment and satisfaction. Contentment and satisfaction erase the need to covet what others have in order to feel like we are somebody! Negatively, the command says, "You shall not covet." We could restate that positively: "You shall learn to be content with the person God has made you to be." That means that part of our calling as people of faith is to help communicate and shape positive identities to and for our people, encouraging them to discover who they are as children of God.

This is really a wonderful choice of commands with which to conclude the covenant because it gives them a sense of closure. Think about it: coveting always involves the worship of some short-term promise—and that is idolatry. Coveting can cause us to look at another person's spouse lustfully—and that is adultery. Coveting can lead to falsifying records or creating false impressions—and that is lying. It can lead to obtaining what we covet by unscrupulous methods—and that can lead to stealing or even murder.

The story of Henrietta Garrett's estate bears that out. In their frantic efforts to stake their claim, many who coveted her wealth and possessions—these alleged relatives—committed perjury, faked family records, changed their own names, altered data in church Bibles, and concocted absurd tales of illegitimacy. As a result, twelve were fined, ten received jail sentences, two committed suicide, and three were murdered. Like fools after gold, the thing they thought would enhance their life in some cases took their life from them. Such is the effect of the covetous spirit upon the human heart.

A better approach for persons who take the tenth commandment seriously is expressed in a story told by the

German mystic Tauler, who met a beggar one day. "God give you a good day, my friend," he said to the beggar. The beggar answered, "I thank God I never had a bad one."

Then Tauler said, "God give you a happy life, my friend."

"I thank God," said the beggar, "I am never unhappy."

In amazement, Tauler said, "What do you mean?"

"Well," said the beggar, "when it is fine, I thank God; when it rains, I thank God; when I have plenty, I thank God; when I am hungry, I thank God; and since God's will is my will, and whatever pleases him pleases me, why should I say I'm unhappy when I am not?"

Tauler looked at the man with astonishment and asked, "Who are you?"

The beggar answered, "I am a king."

"Where then is your kingdom?" asked Tauler.

And the beggar answered quietly, "In my heart."[2]

Contentment, as well as coveting, begins in the heart. The contented heart dwells upon the covenant relationship and rejoices in it. The covetous heart wildly chases after anything that promises satisfaction. Peace and contentment are not so much products of the things we have as they are confidence in who we are and whose we are. Coveting is not so much a matter of wanting things as it is a matter of needing an identity. Living by the covenant offers a remedy to that ailment. And that is no fooling.

■

**You shall be content with who
you are in God's eyes.**

For Discussion

1. What is the root cause of coveting?
2. How is it different from the previous commandments?
3. How is it detrimental to community life?
4. How has life in the community of faith helped you become content with who you are as a child of God? What more could the church do to help you in this area so that coveting is not attractive to you?

■▪

*I give you a new commandment,
that you love one another. Just as
I have loved you, you also should
love one another.*

11

The Test

An Active Love

During World War II, a young soldier struck up a pen-pal relationship with a woman he had never met. Their correspondence began as a result of a book he checked out of a public library. Its previous owner had penciled some notes into the margins of the book. The insightfulness of the comments, the clues into the heart and soul these notes offered, and the beauty of the handwriting inspired the lonely soldier to seek out the woman whose name was written in the book.

The day after he wrote his introductory letter to her, he was shipped overseas. For the next year, the two corresponded regularly. In the process, their mutual pleasure increased with each letter. The man repeatedly asked for a photograph, but the woman always declined. Still, their feelings for each other grew.

Finally, it was time for the man to return to the States. He and his pen pal decided to meet. They arranged a 7:00 p.m. rendezvous in New York's Grand Central Station. He would know her, she wrote, by the red rose she would wear in her lapel.

Shortly after he entered the station, a tall, beautiful blond in a pale green suit sauntered by him. Almost magnetically, the lonely young man was drawn toward this woman with an alluring vitality and sensuality. She smiled a tiny inviting smile at him and even murmured, "Going my way, sailor?" as she strolled past. But her spell over him was broken when he suddenly saw behind her a woman wearing a red rose on her lapel. His heart sank. She was as plain as the blond had been stunning. She was much older and grayer than he, but with eyes that twinkled warmly in a gentle face. As the blond walked away, the young man resolutely turned his back on her beauty and strode to the simple woman wearing the red rose.

As he looked at her, he faced the disappointing realization that this relationship would never be one of romantic love that he had hoped for. Yet he was buoyed by the memories of their letters and the prospect of having a new lifelong friend—one whose wit and intellect he already knew and appreciated from all their correspondence.

The young man introduced himself to the woman with the red rose and suggested they go out for dinner. But the woman just smiled with amusement and told him, "I don't know what this is about, son, but the young lady in the green suit who just went by begged me to wear this rose on my coat. She said if you were to ask me out to dinner, I should tell you she is waiting for you in the big restaurant across the street. She said it was some kind of test."[1]

In some ways, life is a test God gives us. In our responses to the situations and opportunities of life, we give evidence of how well we have absorbed the teachings God sends us. If worship is school in session, the rest of life is homework, not recess. Life is a laboratory where we can experiment with the truth we grasp in moments of communion with our Creator. And face it, sometimes we goof. We mix the wrong elements, and things explode. But when the smoke clears, we must begin again.

The young soldier in the story passed an important test because he was willing to pursue a relationship that held the promise of a mutually reciprocating love, though it initially appeared to be something other than the romantic love he also desired. He demonstrated that he could love for the right reasons, rather than automatically rejecting someone who did not fit his aspirations.

In many ways this young man's test is also our test. One of the things on which we are tested is how well we love one another. Someone once said, "Love is not made to be loved but to be loving." That is to say, love is not some sacred ideal whose beauty we cherish and place on a pedestal so we can merely admire it or have it warm our hearts. Love is an active *verb*. We are to *be* loving. Good intentions alone just aren't sufficient. As someone once said, "We are judged by our actions, not our intentions. We may have a heart of gold, but so does a hard-boiled egg." Houssaye stated it a bit more elegantly when he said, "Tell me whom you love, and I will tell you who you are."[2]

We have explored the Ten Commandments, listening to their wisdom that transcends the ages. Each of the ten advocates principles which, taken together, provide tools to aid Christians who wish to offer a model of community to the world in which we live. Once we have responded to God's invitation to a covenant relationship, these are the basic guidelines for our relationships with God and with other people. They are grace-filled aids given by God to enable us to live as covenant people.

Now for the test, though not a written one! The test comes as we address opportunities and situations day after day after day. To help us know how well or poorly we are testing, we conclude this study of the Ten Commandments with Jesus' words regarding a new commandment. Given Jesus' statement in John 13:34 about giving us a new command, perhaps we should begin referring to the Eleven Commandments. Suggesting Eleven Commandments rather than calling for just one reveals my position on the relationship between the Decalogue and Jesus' command. I don't believe Jesus intended for his command to replace the original ten, but it certainly enhances them. If the Ten Commandments are the components of a shiny new automobile, then the eleventh or new commandment is the key that makes the car purr with perfection and gets it going down life's road.

The Ten Commandments themselves never use the word *love* in their description of the faith community's life. But if we look closely, we can see how important the ingredient of love is to living out the commandments. Furthermore, immediately after Deuteronomy's version of the Ten Commandments in chapter five, Moses summons Israel: "Hear, O Israel: the Lord our God, the Lord is one. Love the Lord your God with all your heart and with all your soul and with all your strength" (Deut. 6:4).

Centuries later, when the Pharisees questioned Jesus about the most important commandment, he joined that verse from Deuteronomy 6 with part of another law in Leviticus 19:18: "Do not seek revenge or bear a grudge against one of your people, but love your neighbor as yourself. I am the Lord." All the law and prophets, Jesus said, hang on these two commands (Matt. 22:34-40). One might say Jesus was returning to the original spirit of the Ten covenant-forming Commandments; another might say Jesus was offering an improved interpretation of them. In either case, what should strike us is that keeping the commandments, according to Jesus, is to be a result of love, not mechanical obedience, learned by rote or driven by computer.

In the Gospel of John, Jesus refined the love principle a bit more when he said to his disciples, "I give you a new commandment, that you love one another. Just as I have loved you, you also should love one another. By this everyone will know that you are my disciples, if you have love for one another" (John 13:34-35, NRSV). It is impossible to love others as Jesus has loved us without keeping the Ten Commandments. I am referring less to the "thou shalt not" renditions of the commands with which we are so familiar, and more to the positive, virtuous, community-building principles expressed by them.

In addition to what they teach about knowing and relating to God, the Ten Commandments have defined some essential qualities for relationships in the faith community. Qualities such as integrity rather than abuse, inspiration for life rather than irritation toward each other, trust rather than betrayal, recognition of and respect for other people's boundaries rather than willful and frequent violation of them, truth telling rather than lying, cultivating positive rather than degrading self-identities.

Those elements were present in Jesus' interactions with other people and in the ministry he conducted in the context of these relationships. Just as God called the Israelites into the faith community by means of the covenant, Jesus came preaching and calling us into a covenant community he called the kingdom of God. Through his teachings, healings, and confrontations, the principles of a covenant community as expressed by the Ten Commandments, plus this new one, occur over and over. These principles were given birth by the love God had for the world. The love Jesus demonstrated, and in fact the love to which he calls us, is a love born from the heart of God.

Now we are being told that if we wish to be disciples, if we wish to effectively live out the covenant, if we wish to pass the test, we are to learn to love as Jesus loved us. In fact, this is so much the deciding factor in the test of life that in 1 John, the writer says, "We know that we have passed from death to life because we love one another. Whoever does not love abides in death" (3:14, NRSV). That is to say, we know we are passing the test when love is an active verb in our lives.

An illustration of this comes from the mouth of a preschool girl who brought her sullen and withdrawn teacher a handful of flowers to cheer her. Then she learned that the reason the teacher was so sad was because her mother had just died. With her big blue eyes and childlike innocence, the girl asked, "Did she live until she died?" Insight streamed into the teacher's life as she realized that there were a lot of people who never love or live while they are alive. She realized that although the grief of her mother's passing was still great, she must begin to open her heart and love again so that she would make love an active verb and truly live until she died.

Yet love has become more of an ideal than a verb, and many of us do not do well on the test. We think we do not have time to love. Active love is time consuming. We think this will only wear us further down until we have nothing left to give. However, recent studies have documented and explained "the helper's high," gained through volunteering. In a book called *The Healing Power of Doing Good*,[3] Allan Luks defines and chronicles this phenomenon as being characterized by an almost euphoric sense of well-being, coupled with a revitalizing burst of energy, followed by an even longer period of great calmness and serenity.

Luks has surveyed volunteers of all ages, both genders, and varying circumstances to find consistently that the descriptions of this "helper's high" remained constant. Instead of finding themselves dragged down by others' problems and challenges, volunteers felt "pumped up," exuberant, happier, healthier, and more stress-free. This "high" persisted for hours, days, or even weeks, after the service experiences. In such cases the people involved were not only passing the love-in-action test. They were also receiving bonus points.

Are we passing the test? How are we loving one another? As you well know, there are various ways and degrees of loving. Some of them are more consistent with Jesus' teaching than others. There is the sentimental, vague "love" some people claim to have for "everyone." There is the love we extend to those like ourselves, or to those who at least have "potential." And of course, there are the types of love we have for a friend, or family, or spouse. Some lightweight loves are limited to attitude. Some love, diluted by manipulation, is conditional. But the best love goes far beyond mental appreciation and good-hearted intentions.

The best love is inspired by the model God has given us through the life and love of Christ. It is not limited only to friends. It is not partial to those who remind us of ourselves. It is as unconditional as possible. The highest love is shown in the words and deeds that present God's love, the gospel message, along with the invitation to participate in the covenant community. Such love is a sign that we are passing the test and living faithfully as disciples of Jesus.

Hear the new command given by Jesus: "Love one another. Just as I have loved you, you also should love one another." Not long ago someone gave me a short writing that states, "[Jesus] never asks me to go anywhere he has not gone, to face anything he has not faced, to love anyone he does not love, or to give anything he has not given." That is an encouraging statement. In addition, we need to recognize all the places Jesus *has* gone and all the trials he *has* had to face. There is not a single person, no matter how plain or unlovely, with or without a red rose, whom Jesus does not love—period. Ultimately, we realize that Jesus' extraordinary love toward us included giving his life for us.

Love is an active verb. As we recapture the spirit of the Ten Commandments, may we also remember this new commandment so that we may pass the test of life in the faith.

■_■

Love is an active verb.

For Discussion

1. How do the Ten Commandments complement the new commandment Jesus gave his disciples?

2. Using Jesus as our model, what does it mean for Christians to love?

3. What are at least three ways your love, and consequently your faith, can become more active?

Epilogue

Israel's area code identified the group's Center and provided the basic principles that guided their relationships with God and with each other. The gift of God's covenant, as expressed in this area code, outlined the core values that guided their life together. So long as the people remembered the covenant, God enabled them to keep the commandments and to live as a covenant community. Though the Decalogue was directed to an ancient group of people, an understanding of these principles can teach today's Christians much about living as God's people.

The concept of a faith community was foundational to Israelite society. It is worthy of our consideration as well. No matter how zealous our faith may be, it is never lived in isolation. God calls "all people," not just "a person" or "a few persons," into a faith relationship. Consequently, personal faith invites us into a community of faith whose Source and Center is the God of the covenant.

Once we enter the faith community, we should expect to live according to the fundamental values that honor God's gift of covenant. Recovering the spirit of the Ten

Commandments helps twentieth-century Christians understand these values and live aright. This means living in such a way as to honor God *and* promote health and wholeness in the lives and relationships of all participants in our faith communities, with blessings spilling over to benefit others living around us.

As the Israelite faith community pledged ultimate loyalty to God in response to the generous gift of the covenant relationship, so also contemporary communities need a shared loyalty focused on God as our common Center. Any community which hopes to achieve and maintain a degree of stability must have a common, uniting cause in some shape or form.

The only legitimate Center for the Christian faith community is the God who calls us into community through Jesus Christ. This is the God whose grace is essential for our entering and keeping the covenant. Without such a Center, any group attempting to "be" the church lacks the very foundation needed to allow a transformation from disconnected individuals to interconnected community. Until we can identify our relationship with our One True Common Foundation as the source shaping our lives together, community will be little more than a memory of ages past and hope for things to come.

As the area code of the covenant demonstrates, commitment to God is only the beginning of the faith community. By its very nature, the Old Testament covenant required relationships between the parties of the covenant. So does community, whether ancient or modern. A group will not become a community unless its members are willing to risk being in relationship with each other as well as with the Center.

If relationships are to exist, it is vital that members of the community reach agreement regarding what is acceptable or unacceptable, important or unimportant. When

God's Spirit leads the church to decide what is acceptable, this produces contemporary equivalents to Old Testament "commandments," providing a framework that defines the community.[1] In other less-crucial matters, personal choice and freedom may operate within the community context without threatening its cohesiveness and unity.[2]

In the process of defining and describing contemporary commandments, we need to remember the principles underlying the original Ten Commandments. We will find them difficult to improve upon. In addition to being a place where a person experiences God's steadfast love, a healthy faith community will be characterized by integrity, respect, compassion, and truth telling. It will encourage contentment and acceptance of God-given identity rather than endorsing desperate efforts to clone the identities of others after our own images.

We live in an age when many people are seeking a stable alternative to their chaotic and often disconnected existences. We worship in a time when many Christians subscribe to a version of the faith that seldom looks beyond an individual's crises and needs. The church ministers in an era when many wonder what practical relevance the gospel message has for their lives. One way to begin addressing each of these situations is to recover, subscribe to, and advertise the Area Code which God issued long ago. It produced a stable, vibrant faith community then, and it can do so now, as God continues to call the faithful into community.

Ten Commandments Plus One, Restated

1. The Lord your God shall be the Source of your faith and the Center of your life.
2. There is no limit to who God is or what God can do.
3. Learn to distinguish between God's desires and human wants.
4. Relax frequently in the Divine Presence, and let God rejuvenate your life.
5. Cultivate real relationships based on honesty and integrity.
6. Enhance the lives of others with random acts of compassion and kindness.
7. Respect the covenant of mutual love.
8. Respect other persons' boundaries.
9. Truth telling shall be redeemed nature for you.
10. You shall be content with who you are in God's eyes.
11. Love is an active verb.

For Discussion

1. The prologue asked: If you were responsible for describing the essentials of the code, what basic values of the Christian community would you define as most important? After studying the Ten Commandments, would your answer to this question be different?

2. Community requires a deep commitment to God and deep relationships and caring between people. What specific changes need to be made in your personal approach to faith in order to live as a community member in accord with the principles of the Ten Commandments? What specific changes need to be made within your local faith community?

Notes

Chapter 1: The Gift
1. Adapted from Robert Fulghum, *All I Really Need to Know I Learned in Kindergarten* (New York: Ivy Books, 1988), 29-31.

Chapter 2: Picture This!
1. Cf. Ps. 135:15-18; Jer. 10; Wisdom of Sol. 13, in the Apocrypha; Rom. 1:21-25.
2. Col. 1:15-20 deals with the supremacy and role of Christ, through whom God was pleased to act for creation and redemption, rather than with a physical picture.
3. Douglas Gwyn, *Unmasking the Idols* (Richmond, Ind.: Friends United Press, 1989), 26.
4. Gwyn, 26.

Chapter 3: Name It and Claim It!
1. Cf. Matt. 7:7-8; Luke 11:9.

Chapter 4: R.I.P.
1. Adapted from Catherine Storr, *Rip Van Winkle* (London: Belitha Press, 1984).
2. Eugene Peterson, *The Contemplative Pastor*, Leadership Library (Carol Stream, Ill.: Christianity Today, 1989), 110.
3. Richard J. Foster, *Prayer: Finding the Heart's True Home* (San Francisco: Harper, 1992).
4. On this further, see also Hebrews 4:1-11; 10:37-38; 12:26-29.

Chapter 5: Get Real!
   1. Margery Williams Bianco, *The Velveteen Rabbit* (New York: Alfred A. Knopf, 1987).
   2. *Economic Justice for All* (Washington, D.C.: National Conference on Catholic Bishops, 1986), 254.
   3. Frederick Buechner, *Whistling in the Dark* (San Francisco: Harper, 1988), 46-47.

Chapter 6: Rack Your Brain!
   1. Patrick D. Miller, *Deuteronomy*, Interpretation: A Bible Commentary for Preaching and Teaching (Louisville: Westminster/John Knox, 1990), 87.
   2. Gen. 1:26-31; 2:7, 21-22.
   3. Compare Eph. 6:4, "Fathers, do not exasperate your children."
   4. Adair Lara, "Conspiracy of Kindness," *Glamour*, Dec. 1991.

Chapter 8: (   )
   1. "Rustlers Stuff Steers in Little Car," *The Knoxville News-Sentinel*, Apr. 11, 1989, A-5.
   2. David Little, "Exodus 20:15—'Thou Shalt Not Steal,' " *Interpretation: A Journal of Bible and Theology* 34 (1980), 404.

Chapter 9: The Real Story
   1. Jon Scieszka, *The True Story of the Three Little Pigs! By A. Wolf* (New York: Viking Kestrel, 1989).

Chapter 10: Fool's Gold
   1. *Encyclopedia of 7,700 Illustrations*, ed. by Paul Lee Tan (Rockville, Md.: Assurance Publishers, 1979), 288-289.
   2. The German mystic, Tauler, as quoted by William Barclay, *Matthew*, vol. 1 (Philadelphia: Westminster, 1975), 260-261.

Chapter 11: The Test
   1. Adapted from Houssaye, "The Woman with the Rose," *Homiletics* 5 (July-Sept. 1993), 41.
   2. Ibid.
   3. Allen Luks, *The Healing Power of Doing Good* (New York: Fawcett Columbine, 1991).

Epilogue
   1. Matt. 18:18; John 20:23; Acts 15:28-29.
   2. Rom. 14:5-8; Col. 2:16; 1 Cor. 7:6-7, 35.

Bibliography

Barclay, W. *The Ten Commandments for Today*. New York: Harper & Row, 1973.

Childs, B. F. *Exodus*. Old Testament Library. Philadelphia: Westminster Press, 1974.

Dumbrell, W. J. *Covenant and Creation: An Old Testament Covenantal Theology*. Exeter: Paternoster, 1984.

Freedman, David Noel. *The Unity of the Hebrew Bible*. Distinguished Senior Faculty Lecture Series. Ann Arbor: University of Michigan Press, 1993.

Fretheim, T. *Exodus*. Interpretation. Louisville: John Knox Press, 1991.

Harrelson, W. *The Ten Commandments and Human Rights*. Philadelphia: Fortress Press, 1980.

"The Decalogue." *Interpretation* 43, no. 3 (July 1989).

Levenson, J. *Sinai and Zion*. Minneapolis: Winston Press, 1985.

McCarthy, D. J. "Prophets and Covenant Community." *Jeevadhara* 11 (1981): 105-112.

Marrs, R. *Be My People: Sermons on the Ten Commandments*. Nashville: Abingdon Press, 1991.

The Author

Jay Marshall is a native of Chatham County, North Carolina. He received his first religious training at Plainfield Friends Meeting (Siler City, N.C.), and there he acknowledged his call into ministry. In 1985 he was recorded as a Friends minister by the North Carolina Yearly Meeting.

For seven years Marshall pastored Edward Hill Friends Meeting (Bonlee, N.C.). Then he migrated to Indiana to serve as Senior Pastor at New Castle First Friends. Whenever possible, Jay enjoys teaching in seminary classrooms. He serves in an adjunct-professor capacity for the Anderson University School of Theology and the Houston Graduate School of Theology and earlier taught at the Earlham School of Religion.

Periodicals such as *Midstream, Quaker Religious Thought,* and *Quaker Life* have published Marshall's articles. His book, *Israel and the Book of the Covenant: An Anthropological Approach to Biblical Law*, was released by Scholars Press in 1993. He has an article on "Rapture" in *The Encyclopedia of the Fundamentalist-Modernist Controversy* (Simon and Schuster).

Marshall holds an A.B. degree from Guilford College (Greensboro, N.C.), with a major in religious studies and a minor in psychology. He received his M.Div. from Duke Divinity School and his Ph.D. from Duke University, specializing in the Old Testament and Ancient Near Eastern studies, with minors in New Testament and anthropology.

Jay is happily married to Judi Marshall, who is an ordained elder in the South Indiana Conference of the United Methodist Church. Their marriage and support of each other in ministry is a living model of ecumenicity.